Perfect Partners

HOW TO BE THE OWNER YOUR HORSE
WOULD CHOOSE FOR HIMSELF

KELLY MARKS

EBURY
PRESS

First published in Great Britain in 2005

1 3 5 7 9 10 8 6 4 2

A CIP catalogue record for this book is available from the British Library.

Ebury Press
Random House, 20 Vauxhall Bridge Road, London SW1V 2SA

Random House Australia (Pty) Limited
20 Alfred Street, Milsons Point, Sydney, New South Wales 2061, Australia

Random House New Zealand Limited
18 Poland Road, Glenfield, Auckland 10, New Zealand

Random House (Pty) Limited
Endulini, 5a Jubilee Road, Parktown 2193, South Africa

The Random House Group Limited Reg. No. 954009
www.randomhouse.co.uk

Editor: Marion Paull
Design: Roger Hammond @ BlueGum and Roger Daniels
Consultant: Nicole Golding

I am really grateful to the talent, patience and professionalism of the
photographers who have contributed to this book and also to Alison Bridge of
Horse and Rider magazine for her continued support:

Amanda Barnes 89; Telane Greyling 204; Kit Houghton 36, 39, 44, 71, 79,
152, 153, 168, 178, 181, 183, 188, 189, 190; Bob Langrish 12, 41, 221;
Kelly Marks Archive 60, 85, 131, 171 (Sarah Dent), 172–3; David Miller 16,
69, 96, 97, 104, 110, 124, 125, 132, 135, 136, 137t, 138, 139, 147,
148, 150, 156, 159, 161, 164, 164, 165, 166, 169, 194, 196, 200–1,
224; Gitte Monahan 9, 28, 29, 51, 63, 118, 145, 149, 209, 217; Simon
Palmer 121, 141; Stephen Preston 49, 70; Anthony Reynolds 146; Hannah
Rose 11; Jess Wallace and Jane Young 6–7, 25, 54, 58, 112; Holly Watts 21,
75, 77; Matthew Webb 19, 27, 35, 57, 72, 76, 92, 98, 99, 100, 108, 137b,
143, 186, 214; Sarah Weston 26; Gail Williams 172

ISBN 0 0919 0087 5

Printed and bound in Singapore by Tien Wah

Extract from The Songs of Horses by Paul Belasik reproduced with kind
permission of J. A. Allen.
Extract from Dirk Gently's Holistic Detective Agency by Douglas Adams
reproduced by kind permission of Macmillan Ltd.

Contents

'I am not a teacher;
only a fellow traveller
of whom you asked
the way.'

George Bernard Shaw

Foreword

Can there really be such a thing as the 'Perfect Partnership' between horse and human? There is no doubt that through the centuries horses have brought innumerable benefits to humans, often giving their lives in service to us. In the modern world, where some might claim that the horse is no longer strictly necessary, we now have the chance to give something back by making our animals' lives as pleasant as possible. Many of us continue to be grateful that the horse contributes his grace, power and possibilities in exchange for our knowledge, protection and inspiration.

In our search for the Perfect Partnership, let's look first at human relationships. Experts have identified the basic qualities needed to make for a successful relationship between two people:

- Realistic expectations
- Enjoying each other's company
- Doing things you both enjoy together
- Communicating in a way your partner understands
- Looking out for your partner's well-being
- Giving your partner the benefit of the doubt
- Respect
- ...And the all-important: love.

While some of these things have to be worked on, it's that last one that tends to sneak up on us or simply overwhelms us. Falling in love with a little coloured horse that bucked people off took me totally by surprise, but when it happens, what can you do? Just your best, I suppose, and what a learning curve one's 'best' can turn out to be!

This book is designed to follow on from my previous one, *Perfect Manners: How to Behave So Your Horse Does Too*. As in *Perfect Manners* I have done my utmost to cover the subjects that will make

'The supreme
happiness in life is
the conviction that
we are loved.'

Anon

the biggest differences for people and the horses that come into their lives. I hope I haven't skirted around any important issues or given the impression that it's all completely foolproof if you 'follow these simple steps'. There is no brain in this endeavour that is more important than yours; the reader's. And it's vital to me that this book is as complete and honest as possible. I've often felt that horsemanship seems to be unnecessarily shrouded in mystery or explained incompletely, and I'm hopeful that the material in this book might provide the 'missing link' in your quest for the Perfect Partnership.

It would really benefit you in working through this book if you could find some supportive people with whom you can compare notes, discuss issues and work through the exercises. They don't have to be horse owners or even riders; people with an eye for detail and a good imagination will be able to make a valuable contribution to a group like this. And anyway, if you're not all like-minded to begin with, perhaps you will be after you've spent some time together! You may already be a member of a pony club, riding club or have friends at your livery yard. If that's not the case, be proactive and put a postcard in your local saddlers' or feed merchant: 'Horse Lovers' Support Group Starting – if you would like to meet up to share ideas, books, educational videos, transport, please ring...'. After all – what have you got to lose?

> 'One of the reasons our society has become such a mess is that we're isolated from each other.'
>
> **Maggie Kuhn**

You may like to try our online discussion group to make new cyber-friends and share ideas: www.intelligenthorsemanship.co.uk. Through the website you can contact one of our Intelligent Horsemanship Recommended Associates, former students who have progressed so well that after numerous assessments and recommendations, they are now helping people with their horses on a professional basis. Having this 'think tank', including Monty Roberts and so many other students and friends generously sharing their expertise and ideas, hasn't only made the Intelligent Horsemanship knowledge base grow exponentially, it has made our time with horses ever more enjoyable and rewarding. I know for certain that this book would never have reached its present state without the enormous amount of advice, input and encouragement from my own 'support group', to whom I'm extremely grateful.

Kelly Marks

Above: Monty Roberts, Ian
Vanderberghe and me with
a foal at Hartsop Farm,
Wilney.

'Never doubt that a
small group of thoughtful,
committed citizens
can change the world.
Indeed, it is the only
thing that ever has.'

Margaret Mead, *Minding Animals*

Feel and timing: let's get them right from the start

1

How often have you heard, 'You can't teach talent'? It's a favourite saying of many horse people who believe that you have to be 'born in the saddle' ever really to know anything about horses. As the daughter of a horse trainer I have to admit that I'm part of that 'inner circle' but I'm willing to break ranks for the sake of horses. It's time for the mysterious club of horsemanship to become available to all.

In the UK we tend to talk about having 'natural talent' or 'a gift', and 'you've either got it or you haven't', whereas in the United States and Australia 'feel and timing' are often cited as vital to good horsemanship. The old horsemen, when they see someone new to horses struggling, tend to suck their teeth (what are left of them), nod their heads and say, 'You see, you can't teach feel,' leaving no doubt that's the end of the matter.

I'm not suggesting that natural ability for certain activities doesn't exist. We're all made up of the same components but we're wired very differently. In some of us, that wiring is particularly suited to abstract mathematics, in others to writing fantastic poetry, or running very fast. Of course, not everyone can be the fastest 100-metre sprinter in the world – only one person can ever claim that title at a time – but we can often excel in a chosen activity so much that those watching might think natural talent is on display. However, no-one for one second should underestimate the amount of work and dedication that acquiring this 'gift' involves. As far as good horsemanship is concerned, it's vital to pay attention to what seem like the tiniest of details in the quest for the Holy Grail. It's also essential to find the right teachers and mentors. Part of the difficulty lies in finding those people – and being able to recognize them when you meet them.

Opposite: 'Somewhere, something incredible is waiting to be known.'
Carl Sagan

One of the things to note about very successful people is that it's hard to know whether they started out with any natural ability at all. Take Monty Roberts, for example. There can be no doubt that he's enormously skilled and works with what seems to be an incredibly intuitive ability, but don't forget that he's been practising his craft day-in, day-out for more than 65 years. You'd expect him to have developed a certain smoothness in that time. It would be wrong to disregard the huge amount of work he's put in by saying that he's a born natural horseman. Similarly, do you think a top event rider such as Pippa Funnel would have the success she has today if her riding consisted of hacking out once a week while chatting on her mobile phone?

> 'A genius! For thirty-seven years I've practised fourteen hours a day, and now they call me a genius!'
>
> **Pablo Sarasate,**
> **violinist and composer**

Not understanding about 'feel and timing' is perhaps the number one reason why people don't achieve the success they would like with horses. Insensitivity to the horse, in the many forms it can take, is the prime reason why horses suddenly do 'bad' things 'for no reason at all'. Sometimes the horses protest dramatically and in some cases they protect themselves by becoming totally unresponsive and shutting down altogether.

'Out of the blue'? Or 'I can't stand this another minute!'?

If a horse is calm at the beginning of a ride but suddenly behaves badly after half an hour or so, the tendency is to think that if nothing is wrong

---

Learning how to behave with horses

I know for myself that attending the Intelligent Horsemanship course changed me dramatically, and I couldn't have achieved the feel I think I now have without that. I always believed it was some sort of inherited gift. For example, my vet is a fabulous horseman. He just walks into the stable and the horses are always calm for him. He is quite clearly a 'natural', while I used to find that in difficult situations I'd be anxious and I'd wind the horses up. It was enlightening to watch Kelly and the team at work, learn how to behave with horses, relax them, lower their adrenalin, and now I know it's possible I do just that. At first it was a bit studied, but now it just happens and I find the effect astonishing. I have been told several times by panicky owners that it's OK for me because I'm just a natural! I'm not, but I can see how this way of handling – just being calm and relaxed – looks to others like a natural gift. I wish everyone knew that this is learnable and although natural aptitude (which some people have) is an advantage, it's not essential if you're prepared to put in the effort.

Ally Sixsmith,
Intelligent Horsemanship student

physically, then it is totally 'unpredictable' behaviour. Why wouldn't he have reacted as soon as the saddle was put on or the bit went in his mouth? Think about it, though. Have you ever had a stone in your shoe that annoys you a little but you can't be bothered to do anything about it straight away? After a while you realize it's hurting, you get mad and say, 'I can't stand this any more!' and you pull your shoe off and throw the stone out. That's how horses sometimes react! Any girls reading this who have gone to a party in four-inch high heels thinking they'll cope will understand. You can stand it for a certain amount of time and then you suddenly realise you're crippled and can't take another step. Or maybe you've worn a pair of jeans that are too tight; it's bearable at first but then you think, 'Enough!' That's how it can be for horses too.

Develop your sensitivity

Horses have a limited way of communicating with humans and if we are insensitive to them, we may not appreciate their ways of expressing things. You have the option of trying to understand them or, alternatively, you can sell 'that impossible horse' – but if you do replace him, you're likely, slowly but surely, to create the same misunderstandings and frustrations with another horse.

'For no reason at all'

One of the clichés of horse behaviour! What's really meant is 'for no discernible reason'. The horse may have a very good reason for his actions. An example of this is Linda Ruffles' horse, Rafferty. Before Linda acquired him he was due to be shot because he kept bucking people off 'for no reason at all'. Linda is an Intelligent Horsemanship Recommended Associate and once she became involved and he underwent some thorough tests, it was discovered that he had a broken pelvis. I think you'll agree that seems a pretty good reason for bucking people off. The people who said he was behaving like that 'for no reason at all' were probably genuine. What perhaps they meant was that nothing had startled him and no one had hit him and they couldn't see a trigger for his behaviour. They may even have had his saddle and back checked but the problem had been missed. As often happens, they decided there wasn't a reason for his bucking because the problem wasn't immediately obvious.

Horses are generally very straightforward. It's a good starting point to assume that your horse never does anything without good reason.

Some people think that horses should behave with unquestioning obedience when it comes to our often bizarre requests, but think about it from the horse's point of view. How would most people behave if you suddenly tied them to a wall and hosed them down with cold water? Or tried to push them into the back of a small van to take them to an unknown destination? Are you starting from the belief that the horse should behave with unquestioning obedience? Are you sure your horse understands this? Did he sign a contract agreeing to do anything and everything you ask, even if he doesn't understand or is frightened? Are you sure it would stand up in court?

Your job is to try to understand the reason behind your horse's behaviour. However clever he is, it's a lot to expect him to be able to see things better from your point of view than his own. If you want to tune in to how horses think, when 'disobedience' occurs it would help to start from, 'Now how can I get my horse comfortable with this and happy to do as I ask?'

Former top eventer Lucinda Green sums it up well in her lecture demonstrations: 'What you're aiming for is a horse that listens to you and is obedient and responsive to your requests, but still thinks for himself.' Unquestioning obedience can be very dangerous; I'd always rather ride a horse that looks twice at boggy ground or a rickety bridge. Remember, just because you've seen another horse do things like jumping ditches or walking over bridges, that doesn't mean your horse will automatically do it. It's up to you to convince him it's a good idea.

Once you acknowledge the importance of feel and timing, you're over halfway there. You will continue to berate yourself for being clumsy and getting your timing wrong, but you are far ahead of those who haven't got the slightest inkling that they're getting anything wrong. Horses are so forgiving they will even appreciate your intention to communicate better and you'll see your partnership improving. Study the theory and then there is no substitute for as much practical experience as possible. Let the horses be your teachers and listen to the feedback they are giving you.

Feel

Two explanations of what is meant by 'feel' are:

1 Sensitivity to the horse. Understanding that a horse is a living, breathing animal with senses and feelings, even if his wishes and fears are not as complex as those of a human. It doesn't make any difference how much you paid for him or whether you spend more than you can afford on his feed and equipment, he is still going to react better if he's asked to do things rather than forced. The great horseman lets the horse think things are his own idea (you can do this with people too: it's all to do with asking questions in the right way).

The Number One Most Important Thing is to know that 'timing' and 'feel' exist and are vital to your relationship with your horse.

2 The ability to feel the horse's reactions through your body, so that you know what he's doing without seeing it. 'I felt the best time to ask for the flying change was when his inside hindleg was just coming through under his body,' for example; or 'I could feel him relax his jaw so I just let out the reins to him a little.'

'Mechanics' and considering natural reflexes of the horse

It's important to distinguish between conditioned, or learned, reflexes and natural reflexes. Some things people assume are natural reflexes, in fact, are not. For instance, some riders think that every horse should know to slow down when they pull on the reins; however, this is not a natural reflex. In fact, it's far more natural for the untrained horse to push into pressure. Much of the training of a young horse is concentrated on educating him to yield to pressure. While some horses learn quickly (because the good rider makes things more comfortable for him as the horse *thinks* about giving the desired response), other horses have to try a repertoire of sticking their noses up or out to one side, and pulling their head round or pushing it down to try to escape from the pressure. This is not 'deliberately being difficult' – the horse is trying to find out what it is the rider actually wants.

Natural reflexes occur when the horse can't help but react in the way he does, and are often based on rebalancing himself if you unbalance him. For instance, if you press the horse in his ribs behind his elbow, in order not to fall over he has to step sideways or move some other part of his body. He will often move his head and neck towards you to balance himself. When you are riding a horse, there are places where your leg, seat and every other part of your anatomy can be that are going to really help the horse and other places they will really hinder the horse. People often seem to forget when leading a horse that if they take his head one way his back end goes the other way, and then they are surprised when their horse damages his hip on a stable door or gateway. You need to think these things through – watch horses carefully – learn how they work!

One of the most obvious areas you can see where people work without any thought of the mechanics involved is when they go to pick up a horse's foot. They don't check at the start how the horse is standing and how his weight is balanced. Then they pull and pull just above the horse's foot, with the horse leaning more and more heavily towards them. They would be well advised to step back and look at the whole horse for a moment. Perhaps they should get the horse to take a step back to get his weight on the legs they want him to balance on. If it's a front leg they want to lift, they should give him a nudge to his shoulder, which would helpfully rebalance his centre of gravity. That's often enough for him to pick up the leg without any other signal.

If you take the time to think through how each and every action affects the horse mechanically, you will make it much easier for him to get things right and make your work together so much more enjoyable.

The rebalancing principle is true for people, too. If you grab hold of a friend's ears and start using them to turn his head as he walks along, pretty soon you would find his shoulders, hips and his whole body would turn as well – so long as he is relaxed, of course. If he is tense,

'A very simple example of feel for me is when my riding instructor tells me to look at the clouds when I'm trying to execute leg yield, for example. It helps me to "feel" better by, I think, removing one of my senses – sight – which otherwise would intervene and try to solve the problem for me.'

Intelligent Horsemanship student Carolyn Bostock

Opposite: 'Invent your world. Surround yourself with people, color, sounds and work that nourish you.'
SARK

or you haven't developed a rapport with him, you might find he reacts quite awkwardly when you grab his ears! Again, this response is the same with horses.

Exercise to increase your subtlety and sensivity, or 'riding by telepathy'

Most horses will look where you look, particularly when you're riding. Gently hold the reins level and turn your eyes to a specific point as you walk along. As you turn your eyes, you may not even be aware of it but your shoulders and hips will turn a little, which will influence your leg position and weight distribution. Forget about the aids for a while. Notice how the horse seems to be reading your mind when it comes to where you should go. If this isn't the case, don't worry. Just keep working through the exercises below and try again from time to time to see whether it starts to develop.

Loosen up, kid – but keep it together

You're never going to develop feel while you're sitting in the saddle as stiff as a board, nor if you're as floppy as a rag doll. You need to go with the flow, move in harmony with your horse. Perhaps you've heard this before but haven't really understood what it means – consuming half a bottle of red wine might have the same effect, but that's not generally advisable. Moving in harmony with your horse means moving enough to match the horse's action without exceeding it. This is often easiest to see at the canter. The rider's pelvis should be perfectly synchronized with the motion of the horse – not stiff and unyielding and equally not artificially forcing movement. You should feel yourself moving with the horse and make moment-by-moment adjustments.

An ideal exercise for relaxing the hips is the scissor-kicks exercise described on page 23. By adding challenges to your balance – such as moving your arms and legs in particular ways – you can make sure that you haven't introduced too much relaxation. If you're at risk of falling off, you have!

The value of 'knowing oneself'

In my experience of watching students I've noticed four main categories that people tend to fall into that work against them developing feel and timing:

- Too heavy-handed, thinking force is going to be the answer.
- Too wishy-washy and indecisive, just 'hoping for the best'.
- Too 'busy', never relaxing long enough to have an awareness of what's happening.
- Lacking focus, so too slow and behind the action to reinforce the horse's movements at the right time.

If you can identify which category you fall into, it will become far easier to develop an effective strategy (towards perfection!).

How to improve feel as a rider

Close your eyes to see more clearly what's happening

In safe circumstances, i.e. with someone trustworthy leading you (if they are really trustworthy, they can lead you from another horse), ride at a walk with your eyes closed and feel what the horse is doing. Have someone watching you and say out loud which leg is moving to where, starting with the front legs.

Follow the movement of the horse's shoulders with your arms

Aim to move your arms fluidly, more like a gymnast or a dancer than Pinocchio or a rag doll. Whoever is leading or lungeing you can tell you how you're doing. Have them change the speed of the walk or trot, and see if you can adapt your arm movement. Then repeat the exercise focusing on your thighs.

Have riding lessons on the lunge

This is probably the number one way for a rider to improve feel. Try to observe from your movements which diagonal you are rising on, or which leg you are cantering on.

Enough is enough

Beware of the tendency to think that more is better. For example, say you start off too floppy on the horse and the instructor gives you some tips on how to become more stable. The horse seems to appreciate it and your riding improves, but if you keep doing the exercises to improve stability, you could find you've gone too far and end up being too stiff. You might pass right through the optimal point in your desire to get even better. Knowing when you've got to where you wanted to go is a key point in the journey.

In canter, your leg and hip will move slightly forwards on the side of the horse's leading leg – start to feel this. Close your eyes, if you feel safe doing so, and try to pinpoint the moment when the horse is in suspension, i.e. has all four feet off the ground. Can you count out loud in

time to the horse's footfalls? (Unless you're riding a well-schooled horse, you'll be saying 1-2-3 very quickly!)

When halting square, feel how high the horse's back lifts underneath the saddle. If it is too high, he has one hind foot too far forward and is not square, but be aware that moving correctly between walk and halt can be a very good way for the horse to engage the muscles of his back.

What to do if you can't feel anything

When the instructor says, 'Can you feel the outside shoulder coming forward now?' the honest student may well answer, 'No,' but most people hate to disappoint their instructor and say, 'Oh yes.' Most people don't know what it is they're meant to be feeling anyway and don't like to keep asking. The instructor often doesn't really know how to describe the feeling and if the student has said 'yes' that's often where the matter rests, with the student feeling inadequate and the instructor at a bit of a loss to know why things aren't improving. (At least there's some feeling going on!) The answer isn't to move on to something else. For part of every lesson, keep working on finding that feel. For instance, say 'Now' when you think the shoulder is moving. After all, you've got a fifty-fifty chance of getting it right!

Incidentally, if you're always getting it wrong, that's against the odds. Chances are that you are feeling something but it's the opposite of what you were expecting. Pay particular attention to your hips and thighs because you will feel the movement through them more than any other part of your body.

This exercise obviously has relevance for knowing what diagonal you're on but can be used to improve feel in plenty of other ways, too. Think about the shape of the horse's back. Why not make a scale from 1 to 5, where 1 is very hollow and 5 is so engaged you think he might be about to buck? Both you and your instructor should give the horse a score. Keep doing this and over time you will find that your score will start to coincide with your instructor's. You could use the same numbering system to develop body awareness. Are your head, spine, hip and ankle in a vertical line? Is your upper body behind or in front of the vertical? Is your ankle in line with your hip, or in front or behind it?

> Your horse will let you know when you're getting things right. Keep listening to the feedback from your horse.

You are unlikely to develop feel if you're focused continually on your horse's head position, or what you're going to have for dinner, so keep drawing your attention back to the task in hand until feel becomes second nature.

Don't get despondent if it doesn't all fall into place on the first day! Just as wine-tasting opens new neural pathways in the brain, so your dedication to this study will slowly but surely open a whole new awareness for you. Once you have learned this awareness, you'll wonder how you ever could have missed so much before!

Positive interaction

When you're making progress and you achieve a particularly good move, ask yourself what was different about it. What did you do differently, how did it feel different? At that moment when it went well, what did or didn't you say to yourself?

Try the scissor-kicks exercise

Working with an imaginative and safety-conscious instructor, move your legs in time with the horse's back legs, so one goes forwards while the other goes backwards. The rest of the body stays as straight as possible. The movement should originate from the hip, not the knee. Don't worry if you are stiff. Keep practising and you'll soon see improvements.

Don't talk when you should be listening

So many of us are uncomfortable with silence. We chatter on to our horses to 'calm their nerves', but whose nerves are we really calming? Sometimes the chattering really is a hindrance as it blocks us from listening to our feelings. On occasion, we need to quieten both our environment and our minds in order to be able to listen to our feelings and our horse's responses.

If you feel that you really must say something, give orders to yourself rather than to your horse, e.g. 'breathe more slowly now', or 'move as if in heavy oil'. Inevitably, if you give your horse orders out loud, you will start to think that he under-

'The quieter you become, the more you can hear.'

Babe Ram Dass

stands and is therefore 'obeying' or 'disobeying' them. This reaction is extremely commonplace and can affect your attitude to what is happening with your horse. Don't be embarrassed to offer yourself encouragement. Wouldn't it be nice to hear, 'You're all right, you're doing fine. Well done.'

Practise, practise, practise

Even if you do not feel that you are naturally talented in horsemanship you can develop 'feel' like you can develop anything else, but that's mostly through a great deal of effort and concentration (but stay relaxed!). To keep yourself calm, practise breathing with your horse. Imagine that you are inside your horse's mind, thinking what he's thinking. Even experienced musicians practise their scales for several hours a week. How would you expect to attain the standard your horse deserves if you don't put in the necessary effort?

Please keep looking

In my showjumping days I remember a dealer asking a new young rider to jump his ponies. She didn't ride very well. She kept asking the ponies to take off too far away from the jump, or got them too close. The dealer didn't seem overly concerned, explaining to me, 'I know she can't see a stride at all, but it's OK because she's always looking for a stride. As long as the rider's looking, she'll eventually find it.' That message has stayed with me. If you ever talk to so-called 'overnight successes', you'll find that they've actually been working at their craft for years. The message is, if you want to be good at something, you can't afford to go through life as if you're in a trance. You must keep looking for that stride – because one day you'll find it!

> 'Look and you will find it – what is unsought will go undetected.'
>
> **Sophocles**

The one-minute rapport-builder

An equine osteopath asked me, 'If you have just a few minutes in which to create a rapport with a horse before treating him, how would you spend that time?' Assuming he wouldn't have time to do a full Join Up* my advice was to use a Dually halter (see page 27) or headcollar and spend a minute or two 'taking control of the horse's feet', i.e. asking the horse to move backwards and forwards. If your horse is particularly bargy or pushy, you may need to spend longer on this.

This practice is based on how horses relate to each other within the herd. There's only one way a horse can show leadership to another in the herd and that's by controlling where the other horse goes. Showing your horse that you can control where he puts his feet is not about intimidating him but reassuring him that you are someone worthy of respect and trust. This method of building rapport is equally helpful for

* Join Up: A method of building trust and respect using body language, discovered by Monty Roberts as he watched horses in the wild. (See *Perfect Manners*.)

nervous horses as it is for bargy horses as long as it is carried out calmly and confidently.

After that, one of the ways to bond with the horse is by scratching his withers and the bottom of the mane. This is where horses scratch each other. A horse can't reach those spots to groom himself, so some co-operation is necessary, and scratching and rubbing here, by horses or humans, reduces the heart and pulse rate. This is particularly noticeable in foals, with an average reduction of up to 14 per cent. Some people say you should stroke a horse with the same action his mother used to lick him when he was born. Try both scratching and stroking and see which your horse prefers.

The one-minute stroking

How often do you think you stroke your horse each week? In these busy times it's rare for many horses to get more than a quick brush over from their owners. It's certainly unusual to hear of riders spending relaxing, quality time just stroking their horse. I have found the one-minute exercise very useful with students who have difficulty getting the horse to follow them in the bonding exercise, Join Up. I ask the students to feel whether their breathing is matching the horse's breathing. As the students are slowly and rhythmically stroking the horses' necks I ask them to feel how they might relax the horse and reassure him. I time them for one minute and when it's up, they try walking away from the horse again in a confident and relaxed fashion. Nine times out of ten the

Above: 'Every compassionate hand is a healing hand.'
Pamela Hanney

Watch and learn

In the fields of music and art, non-experts can often recognize greatness when they hear or see it. Keep watching good horse people at work and, just as you practised getting inside your horse's head, now practise getting inside their heads. When I first met Monty Roberts, I tried a couple of Join Ups and they worked adequately but it was a bit like painting by numbers. Soon afterwards I accompanied him on a trip to Ireland where he did eight demonstrations in a row. I watched and went through every demonstration as if it had been my own, and when I got home and started work again, I found I'd made a quantum leap in improvement. Studies have shown that practising in your mind – that is, visualizing or running through the feelings of the process – can be as effective as real practice.

I believe the reason our students on five-day courses make such incredible progress is that part of the course involves watching and studying each other. It's a major part of their learning. If you watch other people intently enough, it's almost as if you can absorb some of their talent. Try it and see.

horse follows them. Not only is the effect interesting in itself but it's striking that most students think that one minute feels like forever – even more so if everyone is quiet. Comments such as, 'I thought you must have forgotten me!' are not uncommon.

It's debatable whether the value of this exercise is the pleasure it brings the horse or the fact that it relaxes you, the human, making you more acceptable to the horse and increasing his pleasure in being with you. However it works, it certainly slows you down and gives you time to get in tune with your horse – doctors could prescribe this to cure any number of ills!

My farrier was recently shown by a physiotherapist that if you deeply massage any one of the horse's neck muscles, within a minute most will relax enough to half close their eyes and let their bottom lip droop. He finds this invaluable when he has to replace a shoe at the races and has a very hyped-up horse to deal with. He doesn't even have to tell the owner or trainer what's he's doing (good in a laddish culture where these 'soft' ideas may be dismissed). He just starts the deep stroking

Right: 'Horses stay the same from the day they are born until the day they die ... They are only changed by the way people treat them.'
Tom Smith, trainer of Seabiscuit

as soon as he's near enough. People around will often remark, 'Oh, that horse isn't in as much of a state as I thought'.

Look and you will see
Take time to watch your horse in the field. Get a chair if that's more comfortable and maybe go with a friend. Spend at least an hour there –

much more entertaining and rewarding than watching reality TV! See how your horse relates to other horses. Is he a leader? Is he aggressive or just respected? Is he bullied? Explore ideas for yourself. Do you believe a pecking order operates among horses? There are many differences of opinion about this. What are your views on dominance? Again, this is a matter of great debate. What are you seeing with your own eyes? How do you feel the horses relate to you when you go into their field? Do they see you as a dominate being they need to move away from? Perhaps they barely acknowledge you and walk right over you when it suits them? Is there anything you'd like to change? Or do you feel you've got the balance right for the Perfect Partnership?

The Dually Halter

*The Dually Halter was designed by Monty Roberts for training horses. It has two soft ropes that go across the horse's nose and when used on the schooling ring it positions you at the side of the horse's face which is a far more effective position than under his chin. It is obviously much kinder and more practical than a chain which many people use over the horse's nose, or the thinner rope which goes over a horse's poll which can encourage rearing or soreness. It can also be used for riding (it has a similar action to the Western sidepull) and long lining.

Write everything down if you can because it helps you organise your thoughts. I find I learn much more by writing things down. It's worth writing a book just for the valuable learning experience it provides! If you're artistic, sketching can have a similarly beneficial effect. Really study your horse, or all the horses in the field. How do the eyes, ears, mouth and back change in different situations? It's often not until you translate things into words or pictures that you start to understand what's happening. At the very least, try to tell someone else what you've seen, which is another excellent way of helping you to clarify your thoughts.

Timing

This can be defined as identifying the precise instant to reinforce an instruction by rewarding or releasing pressure, or knowing the correct time to ask for another action, as in canter transitions.

How to improve timing

The yes/no game

On my horse psychology weekends we include a game on the first morning which we call the 'Yes/No game'. Two students, called a trainer and a trainee, are teamed together to perform three tasks. The trainee is asked to leave the room for a couple of minutes while the trainer decides the task to be performed, for instance, picking up an article in the room and passing it to someone. For the first task, the trainer is only allowed to use the word 'no' to inform the trainee that she is not doing the right thing. For the second, the trainer is only allowed to use 'yes' when the trainee is doing the right thing. For the third, the trainer can use 'yes' and 'no'. Timing is absolutely crucial. The trainer must learn to speak when the trainee even looks in the right direction. This is the level of sensitivity you need to develop with horses. If the horse even thinks in the right way, you have to reinforce the behaviour instantly.

This game often stirs up a variety of emotions in participants, which can be very revealing. Some people become more and more confused and give up quickly, feeling it's hopeless. Others may be confused but keep trying, i.e. they keep offering a behaviour. This is vital because with no response to reinforce, how is learning going to take place? Then there are other people who may become more and more frustrated, anxious and clumsy, or lose confidence altogether. One person who took part went into a complete sulk, sat on the floor and refused to do any more!

Chewing things over

I turned up at Kelly's place one day. She wasn't around and her sister told me she had gone out to feed the horses but had 'been gone ages'. I thought I'd take a look to see if she needed some help. When I got there she was just leaning over a stable door watching one of the horses eating. I said, 'What's going on?' She looked embarrassed and said, 'Oh, I just like watching them eat.' It was a strange moment for me. It took me back to nearly 50 years ago when I was at Cal Poly (University). I watched a young man by the name of Greg Ward who said very nearly the same thing to me as he watched his calves eating. Greg became a great friend and went on to become a great horseman. Sometimes it's as if life goes in cycles.

Monty Roberts

Watching how the students behave is illustrative of how a horse might feel. Mistakes with timing can mean the trainee won't even look at or go near the place where he thought he got it wrong earlier. What might a horse do if you confuse him by getting your cues mixed up or badly timed? Do you ever notice tail swishing? Head swinging? Yanking down at the bit? Does your horse ever seem lethargic and unmotivated? How wrong would it be to punish the human who just didn't understand what was being asked? Even the person who sulked couldn't really be blamed. It's absurd to say, 'If the person doesn't understand, do feel free to hit him with this whip until he completes the task', yet that advice is all too common with horses.

Above: Floyd and Pie grooming each other – 'Happiness is not where you find it but where you create it for others.'

Anon

Ready steady – prepare!

Now get the picture… You're lolling in an armchair watching *Celebrity Death on the Nile*, or whatever the latest hit show is, totally absorbed, when all of a sudden I shout 'UP!' Even if you feel inclined to obey me you can appreciate your movement is not going to be one of beauty. At best it's going to be unbalanced and lumbering as you attempt to push yourself out of the chair.

Imagine what it's like for the horse if in the same fashion you just order 'GO!' or 'STOP!' – not comfortable. He needs a little warning of what you will ask. It's only good manners, after all.

If I prepared you for the move by saying 'Hey, Jim!' just to get your attention, and then after a moment's pause, 'Up!', you'll have had time to set yourself up to perform the action. Your movements will look so much smoother. Not only that, you'll find them easier to perform and less stressful as well. These preliminary requests often make the difference between an average rider and a great rider. Everything is easier when the horse is set up correctly to do his work. Imagine traffic lights with no amber. You'd have to look out for the red and be prepared to slam on your brakes as necessary. How would that feel? How would that affect your confidence as you drove your car?

When you break actions down into the smallest movements, include the warning. Let's set our horse (and ourselves) up for success at all times. When you ask your horse to go from walk to canter, first be in a position that's prepared for canter. You may raise your chin and look towards where you want to go. Note when you're just walking around normally how the rest of your body tends to follow your eyes and your head. You may take a breath to create that little amount of tension that's necessary and feel the inside leg coming under the horse – perfect! If the transition is not that good, think it through calmly, see if you can work out what went wrong and try again.

Balancing an egg on one end

This is an excellent exercise to develop timing and feel and I promise faithfully it is possible! Some people find it easier than others but if you keep practising, really concentrate, take notice of what works and what doesn't work, then sooner or later you'll do it. The only person I've known who couldn't get the egg to stand up was the one who repeated to herself, 'I'll never do this. I'll never do this.' Probably she was more concerned with what other people were thinking than actually balancing the egg and she quickly gave up. The people who eventually develop good skills with horses are those who are positive, determined, listen to the feedback from the horse and keep at it – just like balancing an egg!

Say what you mean

I have been doing my best to teach feel and timing since I started teaching the Monty Roberts courses in 1995. I keep trying to find ways to get the message across more effectively, more clearly. It brings to mind what Monty learnt from an old teacher of his: 'You can't push information into the brain, the student has to pull the information in for themselves.' In the same way, there's no point in me shouting a lot of instructions at a student who is trying to use rational thought, which tends to block feel. After giving the student a few pointers on what to look for, all I can do is encourage her to learn for herself. Feel is to do with your own senses and is a very hard thing to pass on at a practical level. Your 'feel' centre is located in the right side of the brain but speech comes from the rational and practical left side of the brain. In effect, if I describe a feeling to you, it can become a Chinese whisper. Consider this – the left (practical) side of my brain tries to put what the right side is thinking into words. The left side of your brain picks this up and then tries to translate it into the language of the right

'Friendship consists in forgetting what one gives, and remembering what one receives.'

Alexandre Dumas

side of your brain. It's anyone's guess how the final message is eventually going to be interpreted.

I remember about ten years ago hearing an expert on loading horses describe how 'if you feel the line you are pulling him on suddenly go dead, that means he's about to react strongly – probably rear'. I thought, 'Oh no, that's not right. What he should have said was, "If you suddenly feel a tension coming through the line, that's a sign that he may react or rear."' As I thought about it some more I realised we both meant exactly the same thing but were just describing it differently. Teachers have to learn to make their explanations and descriptions as objective as possible. The other trainer and I would have been clearer if we'd said something along the lines of, 'If you suddenly feel the line has a completely consistent pressure, as if the rope were tied to a brick wall, then…' and so on.

N.B. How to avoid that tension/deadness is covered in the next chapter.

Horses are not connected to Broadband
A slightly delayed response from a horse is normal, particularly in the early stages of training. Eventually the response will come automatically but at first it can be like having a conversation in a foreign language. You may understand, but until you're truly bilingual you will translate what's said in your head and then repeat the process with your answer. In the horse's case, as most of the communication in the early days is via pressure and release, the signal has to go from the horse's skin through the nerves to the horse's brain and then back down the nerve to the muscle to produce the response. Do give the horse that moment to respond. If you're sure he doesn't understand, you can repeat the request a little 'louder'. It's incredible how a person who can take 20 minutes to look through the menu at a restaurant, will expect a horse to react as fast as a pistol when she asks him a completely new question.

How to deaden your horse to all feeling
After some time, continuous even pressure stops creating a response in the conscious part of the horse's brain. Nerves work on a series of electrical transmissions that shoot along the nerve fibres at intervals.

'In our clicker training class we had to bounce a ball and get the click noise at the exact moment the ball reached the top of the bounce, which taught observation and timing. It's harder than it sounds but it was brilliant for improving your timing!'

Claire S.

If you press continuously, you don't allow the nerve fibre time to clear and it will not be ready to receive the next message. The reason this system has evolved is to avoid the brain being overwhelmed with processing sensory information that is neither positive nor negative and therefore has no survival value.

The horse will become habituated to continual signals, i.e. just get used to them and so learn to ignore them. In order to communicate with a horse most effectively by touch – with hands and legs, for instance – give light touches rather than using so much pressure you deaden every nerve response.

Another point on timing

If possible, it's always best to book your farrier, equine dental techni-

CASE STUDY

The effects of timing on behaviour

Such intangible concepts as 'timing' and 'feel' give mere mortals like me an inferiority complex. When I first saw Kelly work it was magic, literally magic – but over the course of time I realized that I was not seeing what Kelly saw. The more I work with horses, the more I do see and, paradoxically, this makes it less magical but more wonderful. I believe that Kelly is in constant interaction with the horses she works with and while she is teaching them she is also learning from them – a never-ending cycle. For this reason I wanted to work on a project that would make me concentrate on the minute details of behaviour as well as the set goal, and develop my ability to recognize and respond to these signs.

Kelly says, 'Reward him for even thinking the right way,' and this made me think about the precision of timing. I set out to train three horses, by means of pressure and release, to carry out the simple tasks of putting one foot on a straw bale and then both feet, employing a different type of timing with each horse – thought timing, action timing and deliberately delayed timing.

From a scientific point of view my research was, of course, badly flawed. I had just three horses to study and the application of the timing could not be precisely measured and was therefore rather rule of thumb. This meant that, using thought timing, the horse was reinforced when I felt he was about to move – just thinking about it. This is actually surprisingly easy. There is always a head movement or muscle reflex somewhere

before the action takes place. Action timing was straightforward. Reinforcement, i.e. the release of pressure, was given the instant the target action was completed. Delayed timing involved waiting two seconds after completion of the action to release the pressure.

The training consisted of four stages – approaching a straw bale, raising a leg towards it, resting the leg on it and, finally, standing with both legs on it. As predicted, thought timing proved distinctly beneficial in a simple exercise such as being asked to approach the straw bale, and as the requests became more complex the advantages were even more obvious.

Could this be because the less immediate reinforcements left the horse less confident about the action required and introduced an element of confusion as the next stage was added? The horse trained with delayed timing spent four minutes displaying a range of behaviours before responding. The delayed reinforcement clearly had no positive effect because it never occurred to him to repeat the action. On the contrary, he showed signs of frustration, confusion and annoyance and I felt it was unfair and perhaps unwise to continue.

The general demeanour of the horses was interesting, too. During thought timing the horse appeared very relaxed and remained calm throughout. The horse trained with action timing exhibited similar behaviour but on occasions showed small signs of frustration, such as raising his head and stepping back. The delayed timing cian or riding lesson earlier in the day rather than later. Some people get tired and grumpy by the end of the day. Perhaps I should say *more* tired and grumpy because there are those who start off tired and grumpy and gradually get worse as the day goes along. Let good timing permeate your whole life. Don't book Mr Grumpy for 7 p.m. when you know he's going to be at his worst.

Plenty of people learn good timing at an early age. You didn't just wade in and ask if you could borrow your father's car or, even further back, just blurt out, 'Can I have a pony?' You planned and schemed, waiting for exactly the right moment, then grabbed it. Similarly, you don't go to catch your horse when the local drag hunt is going by. Learn this and you will see the benefits in so many areas of life.

Make intelligent timing a way of life.

---

horse's head was up and he was clearly unhappy, stressed and confused almost from the start.

I decided to further the research by trying to apply the reinforcement training principles to humans, using a game of chess.

To make it even more interesting, I didn't warn my opponent that this was anything other than an absolutely normal game. I thought it was fair enough. After all, how often do we change the rules for horses and expect them to guess what's happening? With the 'new rules' which only I was aware of my first opponent moved a variety of pieces for about three minutes, looking half-puzzled and half-amused. Then she suddenly reached across and moved my black pawn forward which is what I wanted her to do. When I told her she was part of a study and interviewed her afterwards, she said that when the normal actions didn't seem to work she simply felt the need to try something different and when it was immediately reinforced she understood the new rules of the game. This is exactly what we ask of the horse and again the instantaneous reinforcement of the correct action was crucial.

With another opponent, however, I had to stop the game within a few minutes. As he became agitated it was hard to get my timing right and it was soon evident that he was becoming quite distressed and annoyed. When I interviewed him afterwards, he said that he thought I was just being rude and it was making him angry. I was very forcibly struck by the similarity between his stated emotions and those of the horse that received delayed reinforcements – namely frustration, confusion and annoyance. Could the horse be regarding us, as the chess player did, as ignorant and rude? Equally important, here was the evidence of just how difficult timing can be in the case of intricate movement. We often say how forgiving horses are, but a badly timed reinforcement may unintentionally encourage the wrong action which may become difficult to stop in the future.

A lesson I felt I learnt from the chess study was that simply because we manage to get a horse to do what we want doesn't mean that he necessarily understands it. When we work with an animal, if we become too preoccupied with the goal, the danger is we end up trying to impose our will on the horse and cease to react to what the horse is telling us.

Horses have often surprised me by apparently behaving completely out of character, but now I realize that they probably aren't acting out of character at all: I have simply created a false construct of their character. I think the answer is always to remember that this is a job that is never finished. You can never take anything for granted but must listen to what the horse is telling you all the time.

Carrie Davis, Holder of the Monty Roberts Preliminary Certificate of Horsemanship

The German (non) loader and waiting for God

My first major demonstration tour was to the Netherlands, Belgium, Luxembourg and Germany. One of our stops in Germany was at a major breeder of showjumpers and one of the most beautiful stallions I'd ever seen in my life was brought out – 17hh and just three years old. He had been bred at the place and our tasks were to get him started, i.e. to accept his first rider, and then to load him in a trailer. He was valued at over £500,000 because he was the last of a very special line of showjumping horses, but we weren't allowed to know his name. I think that was probably because the yard specialized in loading difficult horses and they had never been able to load this horse into a trailer or horsebox.

The starting went beautifully and he kept his amazing energy contained. I didn't have the slightest doubt that if he had wanted to jump out of the round pen he could have done so, and cleared it easily. When he came in for the loading, he was wearing a chifney bit – the severest bit for leading available, made of very thin metal with a large plate that goes over the top of the horse's tongue. He had two men leading him, one on either side, each holding an individual leather rein coming off the chifney. I realized he was going to be a fair challenge. Here was a horse that really didn't want to load. The best I could do was to get him near the bottom of the trailer (a start!) but at this point he just slowly sank to his knees. Hmmm…

This seems an appropriate time to mention a piece of advice I'd given my students in the first few years I'd been teaching loading horses, doing the best I knew how at the time. I had been telling them, 'Sometimes, it's just when you're about to give up, that's when the horse loads.' I'd always thought this was a divine thing (choose whatever name is meaningful for you – God, Higher Power, Guardian Angel, whatever). I thought that God, on the whole, knows that I mean well, and would think, 'Hey, she's not really got the hang of this but the girl's doing her best. We'll get that horse to load for her.' That really was how it felt. I mean, I'd be

there, doing my best, I'd finally give up – and then 'for no reason at all' the horse would suddenly go in. Why should that happen?

Well, back to the German (non) loader. There I was, making absolutely no progress. I'd gone through every part of my repertoire and all I'd achieved was this beautiful horse on his knees at the bottom of the trailer. Coupled with this, I'm meant to be talking the audience through what I'm doing at the same time. 'The thing about Intelligent Horsemanship,' I was saying, 'is that if you start with plan A and that obviously isn't working, you need to go to plan B and plan C because there will always be a solution. You just have to think of a way to get through to the horse that this is a good idea for him.' Something like that anyway – it was all a bit of a blur, as you can imagine. Then I looked over at Simon Raynor, who was helping me at the time, and Simon mouthed with great faith in me, 'So what are you going to do?' I mouthed back, 'I have no idea!' and I realized I couldn't help this horse. So I stopped trying. I gave a sigh of what I suppose was relief as I had to accept the fact and as I did so, the horse got up off his knees and walked into the trailer.

The horse taking so long to go in probably had plenty to do with some lack of exact feel and timing on my part. I have improved since then and hope to continue to improve over the coming years. However, what I didn't realize at that time, and took more than a few years to sink in, was that there was more to it than luck or pity from a higher power that made that horse go in the trailer. It was the fact that when I 'gave up' I actually breathed and released all the tension I was holding. Once again, it was not a question of the horse going in or not going in 'for no reason at all'. We have to realize how remarkably well horses can read our every movement and even how our breathing affects them. Every time your horse is not doing what you want, look at yourself first and think how you can improve your communication.

Key points

- Feel and timing are essential to good horsemanship and they are achievable with dedicated practise.
- Your horse is your most important teacher. Be prepared constantly to assess and reassess his behaviour to learn whether you're communicating effectively or not.
- Prepare your horse to make your requests easier for him to carry out.
- Aim to reinforce your horse for so much as thinking in the right way.
- Choose the most suitable time to approach any issue.
- Consider the mechanics of a horse. Make use of the horse's natural reflexes. Use your weight aids with consideration, remember how the horse needs to balance himself and how different parts of his body link to other parts.
- Breathe. You can't feel if you're not breathing.
- Practise. Complete the exercises and allow time for feel to develop. Work towards a level of softness and empathy where you can inspire your horse to action with just your thoughts.
- Make the most of your time with your horse. Get to know and understand him. Keep a journal or sketchbook of your time together.

Above: 'Friendship is a horizon that expands whenever we approach it.'
E. R. Hazlip

'If you want
a kitten,
start out
by asking
for a horse!'

**Naomi, aged 15,
Advice from Kids**

Teaching your horse to be bad – it's easier than you think!

When my friend Donna Penfold wrote to tell me she was training her ponies to be bad, I felt she was being unnecessarily hard on herself. I mean to say – who would really do that? Then I thought some more and realized the answer is probably nearly all of us have done this at one time or another!

Remember that the horse isn't brought up with some moral code that states, 'This is right and this is wrong' and 'You must do whatever humans say because they are the great masters'. Horses make most of their decisions based on comfort versus discomfort, or survival versus non-survival. Any time we talk about a horse doing 'the right thing' we must be clear that this means 'whatever it is we want him to do'.

This is quite a personal matter, of course. You may be quite happy with behaviour that someone else considers appalling, for instance, snatching mouthfuls of grass from the verge. To a degree, it's up to you what you accept as good or bad behaviour but it's worth considering a few points. If you passed your horse on, would someone else appreciate his little 'ways' and think that they were so amusing? You are not doing your horse any favours if you allow him to get into bad habits that other less lenient people may feel need 'correcting'. It also isn't in the horse's interests if you allow him to push you around and take charge in every situation, because what start as minor issues can quickly move up into real problems that can be uncomfortable, or worse, dangerous, for both of you.

> All the time you're with your horse you're training him – whether you mean to or not.

> 'When confronted with a difficult problem, you can solve it more easily by reducing it to the question, "How would the Lone Ranger handle this?"'
> *David Brent in* The Office

It's not what you're teaching, it's what they're learning...

Understanding how a problem is caused can sometimes be a good start when you are working to solve it. Problem-solving genius Edward de Bono calls this technique 'upside-down thinking'.

Ten top tips for teaching your horse to be bad

1 *To train your horse to walk off as you mount* Dig your toe into his side as you put your foot in the stirrup. Be sure to land as heavily as possible in the saddle and always ride off immediately.

2 *To train your horse to buck* Feed the highest-energy food and give the least possible exercise. Choose an ill-fitting saddle and mount when you're feeling nervous and carrying a large dressage whip. Sit to the rear of the saddle, ride into a large open space and ask for canter.

3 *To teach your horse to rear* As for training to buck, feed for high energy and give the least possible exercise. A curb or gag bit is preferable. Create a strong pair bond, e.g. keep him with one other horse day and night. When the other horse is ridden away, become agitated and raise your hands to apply strong rein pressure, applying strong leg pressure at the same time.

4 *To train your horse to bolt* Always gallop flat out in exactly the same place on a ride, preferably towards home. Do not school your horse in any way – he might learn what various aids mean.

5 *To teach your horse not to load* Never give yourself more than three

---

CASE STUDY

Donna's letter

What my ponies were learning when I thought I was teaching them something else.

I had an interesting time with Mair (two-year-old Welsh Section D), Mystery (three-year-old Exmoor) and my very patient farrier this morning. The girls are normally so good for him but then a lot of hard work has gone into preparing them to be safe and co-operative. So why today did they both seem to be stubborn and naughty? Because, without realizing it, I have taught them to be like that.

I have very carefully trained them to let me pick up each hoof in turn and hold it for as long as I want to, for which they get lots of rewards – big scratches, lots of praise. I have been so pleased with them. Now they even visibly shift their weight ready for the next hoof, and often gently offer it up. I thought I had taught them to pick up their feet happily and for long periods – ideal for the farrier. However, it turns out what they

have actually learned is to pick up each foot in turn, so after the near fore is put down, the near hind is next as far as they are concerned. Then it's the off hind and the near fore – none of this putting the foot down while the farrier changes from a knife to a rasp. You get each foot in turn, they say. That's what Donna wants, that's what gets the rewards, that's what we always do!

It took the farrier and me a while to realize what was going on with Mair this morning. He was very patient and amused with her, but then he was astounded when Mystery behaved in exactly the same way. It just goes to show how much cleverer my ponies are than I am, and now I am wondering how many other things they have learned that are not what I thought. Has anyone else done this sort of thing or should I surrender my membership of the Intelligent Horsemanship Association now?

minutes to load your horse. It is essential to be late for the event and to be sufficiently uptight about it. Stand directly in front of the horse pulling hard. A snaffle bit is ideal for this because the joint raises in the mouth, causing the head to go up. Be sure to look him in the eye. If he takes a step forward onto the ramp, he should be hit with a broom from behind. If he runs backwards he should be stroked, told he's a 'good boy' and walked in a few circles before going back to the ramp. Make sure he wears massive travel boots so that he's really uncomfortable and feels like he's drowning in a swamp.

6 *To teach your horse to nap going into the show ring* Sit chatting with a friend, preferably the owner of your horse's stable mate, in the collecting ring for the longest possible time until the horses are called in. Kick on sharply to enter the ring immediately. When your horse seems a bit surprised, kick harder and start randomly shouting.

7 *To train your horse to jig-jog* Always ride out in company with a bigger, faster horse that your horse can't keep up with. Keep collecting your reins up while using your legs at the same time.

8 *To train your horse not to want to be caught* Bring him in to work only, never for a feed. March straight towards him, looking him in the eye. Get very agitated if he doesn't want to be caught but give up quite quickly. Throw the headcollar at him for good measure.

Above: Don't fool yourself you ever have control of your horse – all you really have is influence.

9 *To train your horse to keep moving away from you when he's meant to be standing* Stop what you are doing and stand back if your horse moves away or keeps fidgeting. When he stands still go back to him. This will effectively teach your horse that if he doesn't want people around, he only has to move away or fidget.

10 *To train your foal to be thoroughly confused when he grows up, to find problems with other horses and to have no respect for humans* Overhandle your young foal at every opportunity. Treat him like a toy. Encourage him to put his feet on your shoulders and to lick your nose. Feed him mints from your mouth. Laugh when he headbutts you,

TEACHING YOUR HORSE TO BE BAD

moving out of his space as you do. Allow him to chase you out of the field sometimes.

Most horse owners want their horses to be a pleasure to own and ride but may create problems without realizing it. Be aware of all the common mistakes described above and of how easy it is to train your horse to act in a way you don't want. Sometimes all it takes to stop an unwanted behaviour is the application of a little thoughtfulness.

Who's training who?

My horse Pie received some accidental training once but it took me a while to realize it. Pie lives out during the day and if I have to work late during the winter, a friend brings him in for me and I go out to feed him later. Usually, he'll put his head over the stable door when he hears me coming and I'll go and say hello to him before getting his feed organized. Once I had to go away for a few days on a demonstration tour in Ireland. Although he's done some other demonstrations with me, I didn't think it would be a good trip for him and decided not to take him with me. When I got back and went over to feed him in the evening, he completely ignored me. He wouldn't look at me at all. He just stood sideways on to me, staring into the feed room. The first thing that crossed my mind was that he must be upset with me because I'd been away without him. I naturally explained to him that I hadn't wanted to leave him behind and it was only because I was worried about the ferry journey but he remained unimpressed. I went in and gave him a stroke and chatted some more and then went and made his feed. The next night he was the same but I waited a few minutes by the door until he came over to me. I made a point on the next few nights of waiting until he came over before going to prepare his feed.

Pie reverted to his polite and charming self for the next couple of months. It was only when I had to go away again for four days that I found the peeved look returned and it suddenly clicked how easily people can inadvertently 'train' different behaviours into horses. I worked it out that when my friends fed Pie, they would go straight to the feed room. Pie then was under the impression that staring into the feed room would produce his dinner. I didn't want him to turn into the equivalent of those pre-1950s men you read about with the attitude, 'Hey woman, get my dinner on the table right away!' He soon realized the deal is 'You say hello nicely and then I'll go and make your dinner.'

More sophisticated ways of training your horse to be bad
Both you and your horse should be calm and completely comfortable with everyday leading and riding before you even think about using more sophisticated tools, e.g. schooling whips, schooling aids such as draw reins, spurs or food. In fact, you should think very carefully about whether you want to use any of these additional devices at all. Who says you have to? They have the potential to make your life, and your horse's, unnecessarily complicated. These additional aids are really only for those people who are at a very high level of training. The more sophisticated your training aids, the faster and faster things can start going badly wrong. Here's a real-life scenario:

Left: The tack seller's dream!

- Nice young horse, not flexing at the poll.
- Rider starts using draw reins to get the flexion. It works, so rider uses draw reins nearly every day.
- Unfortunately, now the horse is very much on the forehand, i.e. leaning on the bit, and not going forward properly. He is developing all the wrong muscles in his neck and, to compensate, is starting to change how he uses his body.
- Rider thinks the horse needs spurs and a schooling whip.
- Horse is now swishing his tail, getting irritated and bearing down on the bit.
- Rider decides to use a stronger bit with tight noseband to keep the horse's head up.
- Horse's irritated behaviour gets worse and he starts backing off the bit.
- Rider decides the horse must be told 'he's doing wrong' and gives him a kick/smack/pull in the mouth.
- Horse is now, according to the rider, 'deliberately being awkward' and rider gets a bit tougher.
- Horse gives a buck and the rider decides that now 'he really must be sorted out' and gives him 'a few good smacks'.

TEACHING YOUR HORSE TO BE BAD

- Horse deposits rider on the ground, is labelled 'bad' and sold on.
- Rider buys a new horse but – surprise, surprise – you'll never guess what happens…

Training with the language of science

So that's how not to do it. Now let's be more positive. Horses have an amazing willingness about them. Let's do everything we can to nurture and not destroy that wonderful quality. The horse that is happy to try new behaviours is so much easier to train than a horse that is frightened of getting things wrong.

How does training work? What is actually going on when we try to teach a horse to do as we ask? First, it's important to understand some definitions:

- Reinforcement increases behaviour
- Punishment decreases behaviour
- Positive (+) adds something
- Negative (-) removes something

In other words, reinforcement encourages an action; punishment is designed to stop it. It's important to note that positive and negative in this sense are not meant to imply a value judgement. They are simply used to make a statement and everything is dependent on the situation you're describing. You can't say that 'giving a horse polo mints is a positive reinforcement' because some horses don't like polo mints. You can't say to smack Mr Smythe is a positive punishment if Mr Smythe likes being smacked. You might successfully use positive punishment on your 12-year-old brother, though, by kissing him in front of his friends if he annoys you. You can't say positive or negative reinforcement doesn't always work because if at any time it doesn't work it's clearly not reinforcement.

Stay with this for a minute. Another factor comes into play here, known as 'Premack's Principle'. Dr David Premack introduced the scientific world to the idea

---

Predict the future with Intelligent Horsemanship

All the time you are with your horse he's asking you questions. If you don't answer he takes the answer to be 'Yes'. For instance, you are standing beside your horse and he takes a step towards you. You do nothing, so he understands you've said 'Yes' to that. He starts to nuzzle you. You do nothing so he understands you've said 'Yes' to that, too. He starts to chew your pockets. You throw your arms up and scream, 'What are you doing?' His side of the story: 'Suddenly, for no reason at all, she went completely mad. I asked her if it was all right for me to find some food and she said yes. Then she suddenly changed her mind and went nuts. And I'm not talking pony nuts.' Think through your horse's actions and try to predict how they could develop. Experienced horse people often talk about 'reading the horse'. The more you practise watching horses closely the fewer unpleasant surprises you'll have – once you know what to look out for their behaviours are often very predictable.

that if you watch people or animals when they have a choice, that choice identifies a suitable reinforcer for them. So, for instance, if you enjoy making model aeroplanes, you can be encouraged to do your accounts, say, by promising yourself that when you reach a certain point in the paperwork, you can stop and glue on a wing.

The right reinforcement methods are an excellent tool for managing both yourself and your horse. In the documentary *Whispering the Wild*, in which a wild horse accepted me riding him within a few hours, I used letting him roll in muddy water as a reinforcement/pleasant association. The horse's name? Muddy Waters, of course! As always, though, you have to take careful account of what the horse is telling you to know whether you really are using the right reinforcement methods. For example, let's say a person shouts at her horse if he bangs on his stable door with his front leg. If the horse is banging on the door to get attention, this means he is succeeding in his goal and is therefore getting positive reinforcement. Once again, it's not what you are teaching but what they are learning.

Pressure and release training – negative reinforcement
When pressure from the legs is released as soon as the horse responds, this is negative reinforcement. Applying physical pressure to an animal usually results in counter-pressure, a tendency that has various labels, including the opposition reflex or positive thigmotaxis. For instance, if you apply pressure to an untrained or tense horse, he will move into it. If you pull on an untrained horse, he will push into the pressure on his head with the result that he will pull back against you. If you ask a horse for a lateral move and he's upset or frightened, he's quite likely to press into the leg you've asked him to move away from. So, following on from this, you can see how it might happen that if you use both legs strongly when a horse is frightened or tense, it's quite likely he may go backwards or even rear up.

One of the primary aims in training is to teach the horse to yield to pressure, and many misconceptions exist about how to do it. I read in one old book: 'The skilled trainer maintains the pressure, which is uncomfortable for the horse, until it finally gives in to the pressure. Then the trainer releases it.' If this advice is followed when leading or loading a horse, there is every possibility that the horse may react violently. When you apply constant pressure over his poll, as the horse leans into the pressure, endorphins are released – you can tell this is

'We need to reconcile common sense with "science sense".'

Marc Bekoff,
Minding Animals

happening by a sleepy look that comes into the horse's eyes. He could
even flip over backwards – not good. You have to ask the question, how
does the horse know the pressure is going to be released? Is he meant
to keep offering behaviours in case one of them is right? In any case,
by the time he is leaning backwards into the pressure, it becomes
physically difficult for him to move smoothly forwards. He pretty much
has no choice but to move suddenly, perhaps quite explosively. Nowadays, we know that we should avoid that tension in the first place by
always asking with an elastic pressure, changing angles and releasing
the pressure with the slightest excuse – remember, the horse comes
forward into the release not into the pressure. This also applies to rein
pressure. There is certainly a case here for artistry and intelligence
winning over brute force.

Understanding how the release of pressure encourages a horse helps
to explain more ways in which a horse can be trained to be bad. For
example, if the only way your horse can get you to release the reins
when you're riding is to push his nose down hard, he's going to continue to push his nose down hard.

Punishment
Never punish a horse for trying. You can't reinforce a behaviour if he's
not offering one – figures really.

Stand up for yourself and your horse

I bought my first horse when I was 48. I had no idea what I was letting myself in for. I found a place in a small private livery yard where a girl rode professionally for the owner. All the other horses were expensive – my 14.3 Irish cob was not appreciated for her natural beauty and general plumpness.

The people at the yard soon worked out how little I knew and, to be helpful no doubt, suggested I took lessons with the professional rider and went out hacking with her. On the first day she explained to me the main thing I needed to understand. 'The important thing to know about horses,' she said, 'is that you have to make them more frightened of you than they are of anything else.' In this way she got past puddles, ploughs and over large jumps.

During my first few weeks at the yard a number of similarly useful bits of wisdom were pressed on me: 'What that horse needs is its mouth shut.' 'What that horse needs is a stronger bit.' 'Don't go out without a whip.' On one occasion when my horse refused to go past a parked tractor, three of them came charging out to send her past, shouting and waving their arms behind her.

What did I do? I lay awake every night, knowing there was a better way, worrying because I had a lesson next day and feeling terrified for myself and my horse because I knew we'd both be in trouble. Neither of us could keep a good circle, let alone leg yield. In fact,

my horse had come with a few problems. She stumbled a lot and was stiff. She was fearful, particularly of men, and wouldn't have her head touched. She was clueless in the school.

I didn't want to change yards because there were good things about the one I was in. The horses were well cared for and turned out every day. It was just that I was so pathetic about asserting my different view in the face of all this experience and certainty.

I had already seen Monty and I began to follow his and other leads. I took lessons far from home in riding and the Alexander technique, and I got the back man and the equine dentist in to my horse. I began to get more confidence and told the professional rider that I didn't want her to hurt my horse. It all took a long time.

And then I got a place on Kelly's five-day foundation course. The teaching was great but the best thing for me was finding out that there were loads of people who thought, as I did, that patience and kindness are what work. I have my horse at home now with a flighty young friend. Thanks to all at IH for standing up and being counted, and enabling the rest of us to stand up for ourselves, too.

Intelligent Horsemanship student
Scilla Beamond

The whip

I haven't touched a horse with a whip in at least 14 years, although I have used the Giddy-up rope (made from soft rope that does not hurt the horse; see page 158) or a branch with a few leaves to 'tickle' a horse to encourage him to move. Western riders don't carry whips, preferring to use the ends of their reins to create extra impulsion. This is the inspiration behind the giddy-up – something loose and ticklish can be much more effective than something hard and painful because the horse offers far less resistance to it. However, the whip is designed to be an aid and if you choose to carry one, you must think through how to use it.

> ## 'Hitting means you've lost it. Get help.'
>
> **UK TV advertisement to highlight the problem of domestic violence**

The whip – or a long stick by whatever name you want to call it – can be a valuable communication tool and need never be used for punishment or cruelty. Unfortunately, in practice, this is not always the case. Short whips have limited communication value so are often used for punishment. Dressage whips in the wrong hands may be misused in a variety of ways. In some videos and demonstrations, I have heard trainers saying, 'You just tap with this stick or rope until the horse makes the correct movement,' and a little later, 'You gradually increase the pressure if he doesn't respond immediately.' I have found that when this pressure escalates, which it seems to very quickly on an untrained horse, it is extremely unpleasant to watch and abusive to horses.

Using a whip/stick or any other instrument for pain is NOT acceptable.

The experienced trainer practising this method should know the right moment to stop hitting the horse and will often achieve the desired result eventually. He may cheerfully explain that this is the simple scientific process of negative reinforcement, i.e. the pressure stops as soon as the horse responds. However, when the horse doesn't know how to respond and you're watching him go through pain, distress and confusion, it's often hard to distinguish how it's any different from what some of us old-fashioned folk would call 'beating up the horse'. I have also heard in some circles that 'it's OK to hit a horse as hard as another horse would hit it'. This seems to imply that it's all right to kick a horse and break his leg, something that happens with horses. If it's a joke, I don't get it.

Perhaps a good guide is never to use a stick with more force than you would accept yourself (assuming you're not Mr Smythe). Imagine you are in a dance or exercise class. How much force would it be reasonable for the teacher to use to move your body into the desired position? If she had a cane, would it be all right for her to tap your leg for emphasis? Some people will say yes, and some will say no. If you think pointing at or tapping someone with a stick is humiliating, you're likely to think it's not reasonable for a horse either. If you're a boxer, you might think hitting a horse quite hard is fine. So you have to consider both your feelings and the horse's. Whoever is the most sensitive, or has the lower tolerance has to be respected. In any case, it's clear that if you're using a stick to teach a horse to move away from pressure, or to pick up a leg, you will be doing this entirely in the spirit of communication, and would never use the stick to communicate your annoyance with the horse. If you're thinking 'bad horse', just put the whip down.

Just one more thing – I see much more harm than good in young children carrying whips. It's more for them to hold, it gives them the wrong message about how to treat animals and very soon the pony will become desensitized to the whip (although rather that than they run off), so it's a waste of time anyway.

Ask another way

If you are asking a horse for something and he doesn't respond, it makes sense to make the pressure a little more obvious and so clearer – not painful – to help him understand. If the horse still doesn't respond, the way to help him understand is to explain things differently.

I had a riding lesson recently during which the teacher said, 'Now go into the zone.' I hadn't heard that expression before so I took a guess and made the circle I was doing bigger. The instructor repeated, 'Now get into the zone,' so I realized I'd got it wrong, so made the circle smaller. The instructor said, 'OK, now into the zone.' I had to admit I had absolutely no idea what or where the zone was – please could he give me a clue? We're lucky we have the ability to question our teachers in this way and this very good teacher went on to explain it clearly to me. Let's suppose that instructor had just screamed louder and louder at me, 'ZONE! ZONE! ZONE!' It would have been really upsetting. I could have completely lost confidence in myself and I would never willingly have chosen to be around that person again. It's the same from the horse's point of view – if he doesn't understand, don't simply assume he's stupid or being 'disobedient'. Think of ways you can make it easy for him to understand and then let him know he's brilliant when he gets it right. That is the way for him to want to work with you and look forward to lessons. Actually, it works well for most of us.

(By the way, the zone was meant in this instance as the period between trot and walk.)

How whips/long sticks can be used fairly and correctly

Some long sticks can be used as an extended arm. Putting a false hand on the end of a cane can be useful for educating a horse not to mind

Just following orders?

Never let anybody bully you into bullying a horse. In a chilling documentary on Nazi Germany, people were interviewed on how they felt about operating the gas chambers, murdering hundreds of people at a time. The general consensus was 'we were just following orders'.

being touched all over, particularly if he kicks out. The false hand accustoms the horse to having his legs touched while the handler remains in a safe position.

Traditionally, the dressage whip is seen as an energiser, or as a signal to move forward. A light touch brings the horse's attention to a particular part of his body that you want him to move and another traditional use of the schooling whip is to reinforce a sideways leg aid, or to teach one in the first place. On the ground, you can teach the horse to move away from you by touching lightly on the flanks. When on board, ask the horse to move away from a nudge with the leg, and if he doesn't respond, pair this with a light touch from the dressage whip to help him understand.

The short whip

As the giddy-up rope isn't allowed in competition, let's look at how we might create some energy in the very laid back horse when only a short whip is allowed. The relaxed horse has many advantages but when you want to compete around a big round of showjumps, say, you'll probably feel better if you know he is awake and going forward. Don't use the whip for pain so he starts to hate and resent jumping and competitions. What you could do before going in the ring is trot him around at a good pace and feel the excitement rise in yourself, so he starts to pick up on that. You could smack your boot a couple of times if he feels a bit dull, just so the noise picks him up. It's like saying, 'Come on! Let's go!'

Do calculate carefully what's best for your particular horse. With Pie everything is aimed at keeping him as calm as possible before going into the ring. Yet with our other horse, Floyd, my niece Daisy needs to 'raise the excitement' when the jumps are getting a bit bigger. Floyd can jump big fences easily but has a tendency to be on the slow side. Daisy trots him roundly briskly before going in the ring and

> 'Our kind may be able to bully other species, not because we are good at communication but because we aren't.'
>
> **Elizabeth Marshall Thomas**

Make it easy for your horse to do 'the right thing'

- *Horse doesn't want to go in horsebox*
  Lead another horse in first, make the horsebox as inviting as possible, put solid panels behind the horse in the initial stages so he gets it right – tell him he's a genius.
- *Horse doesn't understand to back up from rein aids*
  Ask someone to stand in front of him and gently push him back at the same time as you apply the aids.
- *Horse doesn't want to stand on wooden bridge*
  Get off and lead him on to it, tell him he's brilliant, then get on and ride him across the bridge. Ask a friend to lead him across to start with until he gets confident – tell him how brave he is.

pushes him on strongly with her legs after each jump to keep him moving on.

It may seem odd that two horses can be so different but think about people. If you ever go to a Monty Roberts demonstration, try to catch sight of Monty just before he goes into the arena at the start. He has a warm-up routine that involves running up and down and swinging his arms. Then he'll jog into the arena. If I did that it would wind me up so much I'd probably run smack into the side of the round pen! When I do demonstrations I'm the complete opposite. I prefer to stand quietly on my own beforehand. I don't want to speak with anyone for a minute or two. I concentrate on breathing out, shoulders down, and keeping as relaxed as possible.

It's just as important to know yourself as it is to know your horse. Some people can carry a whip and there's not a moment's doubt that it's going to be detrimental to the horse. This may be you. Ask yourself if you are always in charge of your emotions and so wouldn't misuse the whip, or whether using it may be masking other problems with your horse that you should be addressing directly. For example, are you are using a dressage whip to 'produce more energy' when the real issue is that your horse needs a diet and living conditions that will give him sufficient energy to use? Personally, I would completely trust myself with a whip, although I don't happen to carry one at the present time – however, if I were to carry horsefeed in my pockets I would find it an enormous temptation not to give every horse I met some little titbit (a very bad idea) which brings me on to my next subject…

Positive Reinforcement – clicker or food training

One way of letting the horse know that he's done the right thing, i.e. what you want him to do, is to get him to associate a certain noise with food. This may be a distinctive 'click' sound or even merely saying 'good boy' clearly. You can reinforce the correct response or action the instant he gets it right by making the noise and he knows that the food treat will follow shortly. This is called a 'conditioned' or 'learned rein-forcer' – it's not normal/natural for a horse to think that a sound is a good thing. He has learned that it is, in this case, through training.

Tip: With clicker training, always feed the smallest amount of food you can get away with!

You should not be trying to do this with any animal (this method isn't just used with horses) until you have success-fully trained a human being to do three separate tasks by the use of a specific sound. Try it out and practise your timing with a forgiving friend. Some of the learning theory that you're encouraged to explore will be of excellent value in all your training.

However, using food in this way can encourage behaviour for which you may not be prepared. What often happens is the horse goes through a 'mugging' stage. He sees you as the source of treats, particularly if they come from your hand, becomes pushy and keeps asking you for food. Another thing that often happens is that as the horse progresses and becomes highly motivated, he starts to offer previously trained behaviours to try to get the food. It is important not to reward these no matter how wonderfully he performs. Click and reward for behaviour you have asked for only and ignore unasked-for actions.

One of my least fond memories of a horse I worked with in a demonstration was a six-year-old Andalusian stallion that had been taught to do the Spanish Walk from the ground with the use of treats and a long whip. 'He got so clever, though,' the owner said incredulously, 'because then he just kept doing his Spanish Steps at you so we had to keep giving him the food or he would get angry.' Into the demonstration arena walked this admittedly gorgeous looking creature that would charge you, striking out and grabbing at any part of your anatomy he could get to with his teeth. Not the intended result of the training, I'm sure!

For my first experiment with clicker training I used Floyd, a sensible, generally well-mannered horse that I bought for Daisy to ride in Working Hunter competitions and for friends to ride out when they visit. When Floyd first arrived with me he had the habit of nodding his head up and down all the time when he was standing still. So we checked his saddle, back and teeth to rule out discomfort. It would clearly be wrong to 'punish' him in some way if he was uncom-

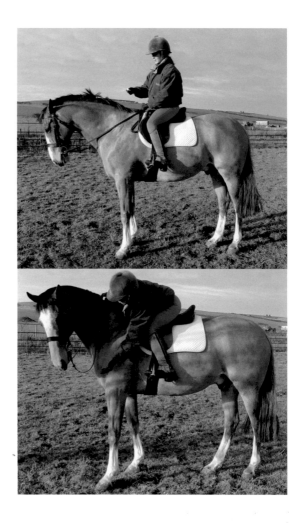

Above, top and bottom: My niece Daisy using the clicker with Floyd – 'Notice the smallest change, the slightest try, and reward it.' This doesn't just apply to clicker training, of course.

fortable. Equally, it's not acceptable to mask pain by using positive reinforcements. The cause of the problem had to be identified and eliminated before we could deal with the nodding, which by then had become a habit.

Working with Linda Pearson, who is experienced with clicker training, we taught Floyd that when he held his head still and stood nicely with his ears forward he would get a click and a treat from the rider. The rider would alternate the side the treat came from, which was good exercise for his neck as well. The beauty of this was that he wasn't encouraged to mug people on the ground for the reward. Occasionally

Confusing the horse

I have trained my mare to rear by clicker. It is something I wanted to do for a long time but I put it off. My horse never rears under saddle but has a lovely balanced rear in play and I was impressed by how quickly she learnt to do it on command in only a few minutes.

However, that was yesterday. This morning, I wanted to test out my mare's new impressive trick to ensure that it wasn't a fluke. So I groomed her and then led her in a headcollar to the manège. Unusually, she jogged all the way. I let her go in the manège and she stuck by me like glue. I did a couple of her usual tricks, such as 'wait' and 'back', which she did. Then I turned to her and said 'up', gesturing with my hands and schooling whip, and up she went into a perfectly controlled impressive rear. I did it again, and again she obliged. Impressed, I thought now was the time for an audience and so I called my friend. By the time my friend arrived, though, my horse was rearing left, right and centre WITHOUT the command, and right next to me. As I didn't click and reward her, she became more and more worked up. She did it again on command and I clicked her. Then I thought I had better leave it there and so got a jump out to distract her, as by now she was leaping about and bucking and play-kicking out at me. Not very nice! I set up the jump and tried to

send her away with my whip but she wasn't having any of it. All she wanted to do was rear and rear and rear. I was shouting 'NO!' every time she did it and trying to send her to the jump. In the end, she got really frustrated and exasperated and turned round and kicked me. She has never ever done that before and I was lucky she didn't break my leg. I shouted 'NO!' at her and left the manège immediately, leaving her alone, which she hates, to think about what she'd done. Then I realized – it was all my fault.

Firstly, she was already full of it before entering the manège, so I shouldn't have done anything exciting with her.

Secondly, I realized to my horror that I used the same arm signals to send her to a jump as I did to get her to rear. All that was different was the voice command. So she thought I was telling her to 'rear, rear' and when she did, I was shouting 'No!' at her rather than giving her a treat. In her utter frustration she thought, 'Sod her!' and kicked me. Doh!

Thirdly, I had overdone it. She loves exciting things and is the same with jumping. I have to forget about the rearing until another day when she has been worked and is relaxed.

Fourthly, only give the command to rear at a safe distance!

he'd look round hopefully at the rider. Also, if he offered the behaviour when it wasn't asked for, there was no harm done. It just meant that Floyd stood beautifully still with a hopeful expression on his face for longer and longer periods.

Key points

- You are teaching your horse all the time, whether you mean to or not.
- Learn to recognize when you've accidentally taught your horse the wrong thing and take responsibility for it.
- If your horse is behaving badly, ask yourself, 'How could I have trained him to do that?'
- The only way a horse knows what is 'right' is by whether the action results in a reward/comfort/safety.

There is some good news. After this disaster, I decided to tack her up and ride her as she obviously had excess energy. She has never ever gone so well under saddle – absolutely magnificent and the most perfect manners. Phew!

But now someone has said that what I have done was stupid and that she could end up doing it in all kinds of circumstances and harm me or someone else who is handling her, and I can see their point. I am fairly confident that if I don't do this for a while and never reward an uncommanded rear, she will cease to do it. In fact, it does seem to be the way she learns because every time I teach her something new, she goes overboard, performing the action uncommanded, in the hope that it will be rewarded. When it isn't, she gradually stops doing it unless commanded. I am hoping that it will be the same thing with the rearing. What do you think? Has anyone else ever taught this? Any advice?

Sally Bruce

Let's face it, we all make mistakes. I was impressed by this horse owner's willingness to look for the problem in herself rather than the horse and how quickly she saw that she was responsible for confusing the horse.

- Whether using negative or positive reinforcement, be careful to deal with the real issue and not just the symptoms. Your horse must be in good shape physically and on the right food, exercise and general welfare regime.
- Have the best possible support when using training tools with which you are not familiar. Get to know the downsides as well as the upsides.
- Whipping a horse because he is frightened or doesn't understand means you are not thinking intelligently about the situation. You should find ways to manage your anger before even thinking about going near a horse (or your family).
- With food/clicker training, be careful to reward requested behaviours only.
- Be careful when choosing what behaviours to teach.

'Anyone who has never made a mistake has never tried anything new.'
Albert Einstein

Mirror, mirror in the stall

The frustrating fact is that you can't impress a horse by telling him you earn £225,000 a year and have a bachelor's degree in sciences. You can scream at him, 'Don't you know who I am?' as much as you like but you're wasting your time. If you don't inspire confidence in your horse and give him good reasons for doing as you ask, the only acknowledgement you're likely to get is as the 'idiot who pays the bills'. The horse's honest responses are very quick to show up our weaker spots. I have heard the trials and tribulations of keeping horses described as 'character building', but is this character they are building the one we'd really choose for ourselves? Horses can be our greatest teachers but this only works if we come out of the trance-like state that many of us allow ourselves to operate in. Allowing life just to happen may feel like the easy option, but is it the most fulfilling?

Life can be so interesting once you become fully engaged with all that's going on, and the same goes for listening to the feedback you get from your horse. Let's suppose you fill out a form explaining how you look after your horse and ask whether the recipient thinks you're doing a good job. If you included a stamped addressed envelope and perhaps a donation, you might even get a letter back with a piece of paper saying, 'This is to certify that Mary Jones is a very good horse owner.' Would that have any value? Absolutely not! Ultimately, only your horse can tell you if you're getting things right or not. Is he enjoying great health? Is he happy to be in your company? Can you catch him, lead him to the stable, put his saddle and bridle on, get on him and ride him pretty much anywhere in complete safety and comfort? Yes? Mary Jones, you must be doing something right. However, keep on reading this book. It might enable

> 'To love oneself is the beginning of a life-long romance.'
> **Oscar Wilde**

you to discover just what it is you're doing right, and then you'll be able to explain it to others and help them find success as well!

The corporate world has taken to heart the message of the horse giving honest feedback, perhaps more than the general horse community. I receive frequent requests from various companies interested in having their key executives spend a day at the stables and learn some of the art of 'horse whispering'. A participant on one such seminar told me, 'I think people don't really respect me because of the way I look.' Curiously, the horse he was assigned had been attentive with other people but wandered off during the session to nibble some hay. The participant was able to look at this objectively rather than from the average horse owner's point of view ('this is a disaster – my horse doesn't love and respect me!'). He realized that, assuming horses don't judge us on our appearance (and I don't remember Black Beauty mentioning it), it was what he was doing that was causing ambivalent feelings in others. How he thought about himself and others and how that translated into how he used his body caused the horse to react as he did. Those little clues that every single one of us unwittingly gives away – the horse had told him honestly. It was a very positive experience for that person because once he was aware of what he was doing, it was easy enough to work on his feelings and body language for a more positive outcome.

One of our very first corporate days was with the company Microsoft. At the meeting they held the same evening, participants reported feeling 'amazingly positive about the future' and said that they had 'learned the value of honest communication' and they 'truly under-

---

What would your horse say about you if he could speak?

I'd want horses to describe me in the way *Black Beauty* depicts John Manly: '...he was so gentle and kind, and seemed to know just how a horse feels; and when he cleaned me he knew the tender places and the ticklish places; and...never stirred up any ill-temper.'

Then later: 'Spirited horses, when not enough exercised, are often called skittish, when in fact it is only play; and some grooms will punish them, but our John did not; he knew it was only high spirits. Still, he had his own ways of making me understand by

the tone of his voice or the touch of the rein. If he was very serious and quite determined, I always knew it by his voice, and that had more power over me than anything else, for I was very fond of him.'

While I don't particularly advocate relying on tone of voice to convey meaning to a horse, the spirit of this appeals to me – and I know *Black Beauty* uses too many semicolons but he was pretty literate for a horse.

Recommended Associate
Nicole Golding

---

stand now that if I don't lead, the horse can't follow'. It brought home to me how lucky we regular horse people are to have the benefit of these insights virtually every day!

Do be aware, however, that you can take this a little too far. The idea is that horses to some extent reflect our actions and provide information that we can look at to see how it might relate to our lives, but they aren't soothsayers or oracles. Perhaps the horse that wandered off had simply lost interest by then, or was feeling hungry. Whatever the reason, it provided the opportunity for the seminar participant to question what it was about his attitude or behaviour that could have triggered the response in the horse. He was able to identify all sorts of possible explanations and thus find positive things that he could work on. Looking at himself honestly revealed those insights. The horse didn't provide the answers, just a framework for discovering them. The key point was that the horse behaved differently with other people, which suggested, but didn't prove, that it was something the man did that caused the horse to move away.

A woman who attended one of our five-day foundation courses mentioned in the introductory session that she was at quite a crossroads in her life. She wanted to work with horses but her partner was not in favour of it. Now it seemed that every time she was about to go off and do something for herself, her partner would become ill. The same thing had happened this time but she had arranged for someone else to look after him and come anyway. She was feeling a bit shaky. A couple of days into the course she did a Join Up with a pony that had been very calm with a couple of other people who had worked with him. With her, he was jumpy and unsettled, and ignored her requests to change direction. A few people mentioned that they thought it might be the pony responding to her inner turmoil. In fact, it was the wind blowing the trees behind the round pen wall

Above: 'I've spent most of my life riding horses. The rest I've just wasted.'
Anon

Remember that although horses may hold up a mirror to our behaviour, they're not doing it with the intention of making us look stupid or brilliant. If you find that you're annoyed because the horse is showing you up, just pause for a moment. As Olympic dressage gold medal winner Kyra Kryklund says, 'No horse stands in his stable ... contemplating the best way to irritate his rider in the next riding lesson.'

that he didn't like. We remembered that he was often unsettled in this particular pen if the weather was windy so we changed pens and he responded calmly. So look at the feedback, but do be sure to evaluate it carefully.

Looking for your first horse

When looking for your first horse or pony, in many ways you want to look for a character as deliberately as possible who is not going to mirror you. It's so often a recipe for disaster and yet suburban myth number 687 is still trotted out: 'They can learn together' – eek! If you are new to horses and lack confidence, go out of your way to find an older, sensible, confidence-giving horse.

Horses seem to love a leader, and by that I don't mean someone who bullies and dominates: that's a sign of weakness, not strength. There has been debate in the horse world about whether the human should act as the 'dominant' or 'Alpha' horse. These terms can be confusing or at least a turn-off

Above: 'There can be no friendship when there is no freedom.'
William Penn

to many people. If you were employing people to work for you it would be slightly bizarre and I'm sure unsuccessful, to suggest you have to dominate them. If you think more in terms of acting confidently, consistently, competently and calmly you'll be on the right track. The next

A wake-up call

I was rather surprised at a Monty demo when a very attractive young woman whose face I vaguely knew but could not place, rushed up to me, gave me a long hug and thanked me for changing her life.

My partner Nicole was listening with a slightly raised eyebrow, so I asked her to explain what she meant. Earlier in the year, she had been on a Weekend Perfect Manners Course, and we had gone through the video of her final Join Up. It had gone all right but she had found it very hard to make her bargy horse move away from her, or even get his attention. Her body language was very uninspiring. It seemed to give away a lack of inner resolve, as if she didn't really feel he should do what she was asking. Anyway, it was the last day of the course and she and her partner packed up her horse and went home. They were just about to unload at the other end and she asked her partner to do something quite simple, like move the trailer forward a foot or two so it would be easier for her horse to get out. Her partner completely ignored her and she had a sudden realization that, like her horse, her partner saw her requests as being completely inconsequential. 'When I saw myself on the video, I could really see why,' she said. 'It was like I wasn't there. I hadn't realized I looked like such a victim.' Thinking about her life, it dawned on her that she was actually in quite an abusive relationship. There and then she told her partner that it was over, she deserved more respect, and she wouldn't be pushed around any more. She walked out of the relationship and never went back. She also started being more positive with her horse and he stopped pushing her around, too. She said, 'I had no idea until I saw myself on that video what my body language was saying about me. I looked such a doormat – unable even to get my horse to move. That was the biggest wake-up call of my life.'

Of course, I had not changed her life – she had. I had helped to create a space for her to make that discovery in a supportive and non-judgemental environment. As she introduced me to her new boyfriend, I couldn't help but think how profound an effect horses, and especially this kind of horsemanship, had made on my life, too.

Recommended Associate Adam Goodfellow

time you panic about something, pause and think, 'I know, I just have to do something beginning with "C"'!

People who have a mission – which is just a name for goals they believe are of great importance – can inspire people and horses to work with them through their enthusiasm alone. This is unlikely to be the case if you are lacking in conviction and are hesitant and unsure.

During a recent demonstration tour I was able to illustrate quite easily the effects of a handler's intention. By 'intention' I mean the raising of your internal energy by strongly focusing on the effects you want to achieve. While I was long lining, I would let my energy drop and my body language become tired. I would droop my shoulders and look at the ground, making all my limbs feel heavy. I'd talk like Harry Enfield's Kevin the Teenager. Almost invariably the horse would slow right down, maybe even stop, even though I was still asking him to move. Then I'd suddenly become high-pitched and squeaky, like a Jack Russell on espresso coffee, wave my arms around jerkily, rise right up on my toes, and the horse would immediately spring into action, looking alarmed. Some horses responded more dramatically than others but none of them failed to notice. Obviously, the ground you want to tread is somewhere in the middle, with the ability to raise or lower your energy from there.

The ambivalent rider is likely to have an ambivalent horse and external aids aren't going to make the slightest difference if there isn't a change of attitude as well. However, watch a person who has a passion for, say, eventing or showing or endurance riding and you'll see that their horses positively shine, giving every appearance of loving those sports as well. Some horses literally give their lives for the sport. They weren't born brave or vain or with a desire to win competitions. It's as if they become an extension of their owner. Perhaps that's why we become so enamoured of horses – your horse is an extension of yourself, but is faster, stronger and more beautiful. What more could your ego ask for?!

Above: Winning on Swing Through at Devon and Exeter – 'Wheresoever you go, go with all your heart.'
Confucius

If you haven't got a burning ambition in the horse world, if you're quite nervous of riding or of horses in general, or even if you're generally unsure of yourself, there's no reason at all to give up hope. It's an excellent chance to build up your personal life at the same time as you build up your horsemanship. Your horse isn't necessarily looking for brilliance. Honesty is an important starting point for the perfect partnership. Be clear and honest with yourself and your horse about what it is you really want to do. If you don't really want to jump your horse over fences, that's fine. Be honest and don't attempt jumping until you feel absolutely ready, if at all. A good measure is when you can visualize and/or feel yourself confidently jumping the fences and it feels like fun. Don't let someone tell you that your horse needs hitting in order to jump when you know full well he's not jumping because *you* don't truly want to jump.

Often, behaviour by a horse that is labelled 'bad', e.g. refusing jumps, running away from frightening things, being suspicious, just means he's protecting you because he feels you need protecting. Do you think he doesn't notice that you approach the jump with one hand over your eyes, the other clenched tight on the reins, whimpering, 'Oh my God, we're going to die'?

Shannon

After suffering a particularly bad riding accident, which resulted in an operation followed by a long stay in hospital, I was very nervous about riding again. When the time came that I was able to get back into the saddle, the only equine I would trust to ride was my own pony, Comet. Although he could at times be a bit of a live wire, I knew that he was safe, and at least he wouldn't deposit me on the floor. So that was the way it stayed for many years, with me just taking Comet out for quiet hacks around the fields and never wishing to get on another horse.

When Comet died at the grand age of 30 years, I was devastated. After 23 years of owning Comet, suddenly having no pony to look after left a huge gap in my life. I wanted another pony to love and care for, but I didn't know if I could ever regain enough confidence actually to ride another pony. Then a friend told me about Shannon. She was a riding school pony. Due to an injury she had sustained when she slipped on an icy patch and fell, she needed a home where the most work she would have to do was to go on gentle hacks and where she would just generally be able to take life easy. Shannon, I was told, was completely bombproof. So I went to see her, fell in love with her and bought her.

Although I was very nervous of riding her when I first bought her, Shannon looked after me and was quite happy to walk quietly along the local bridle paths, despite having a quivering jelly for a rider on her back. Shannon never put a hoof wrong. Even in situations where I would tense up and expect something awful to happen, she always remained steady and calm.

Over the past seven years of owning Shannon, I am pleased to say that some of my confidence has returned. The thought of galloping across an open field – something I would have done with absolute delight in my youth – or getting on a strange horse still turns my legs to jelly but Shannon never attempts to go any faster than I ask her to. Even in the biggest of fields, she is happy to stay at a steady walk and never even thinks about 'taking off' with me. I have also discovered that Shannon is a wonderful driving pony and again her steady, calm nature makes her a pleasure to drive. With Shannon in harness I am 100 per cent confident, and my confidence when riding gets a little better every time I put my foot in the stirrup on Shannon's saddle.

Oh, Shannon does have her moments. She can be cheeky at times, especially when she wants me to give her a scratch on one of her many itch spots, and she is quite a character in her stable, but she has the most wonderful, kind, generous nature. On the many occasions when I ride her and obviously confuse her with my dithering attitude, she proves that has a very forgiving temperament. Shannon is a pony in a million and I wouldn't part with her for the world. In Shannon I have found my 'Perfect Partner'.

Hazel Ann Johnson

If you really do approach a fence like that, you don't need the horse to let you know. You'll have worked out for yourself that you're nervous, or maybe your friends will have mentioned it to you. But once you've examined the feedback horses are giving you about yourself and your handling of them, what's the next step? How do you get the sort of feedback you would like?

Once you realize it's your responsibility to protect the horse, his confidence will rise massively because he will be relieved of making all the decisions. Imagine you are taking a young child through some spooky woods. Wouldn't you pretend that you weren't scared at all for the child's sake? Exactly.

Take responsibility

Why not write down a list of ideal qualities? If you met Black Beauty, what would you like him to say about you? That you're fair, patient, considerate, calm, consistent, skilful? Experience shows that horses respond well to these qualities but equally these attributes may be of no benefit to you if you're trading futures and options on the stock exchange. If you have a job that requires different attitudes from those you need to display around your horse, you'll have to find a way to bridge the two.

Working with horses can often bring to the surface any problems that you've been unwilling to face up to. At times, horses seem to have a built-in sensor that enables them to find you out. Perhaps that's another of their attractions to us. Having the appreciation of a creature that truly knows you is extremely flattering, although it can have its drawbacks. Go to the stables or field in an agitated state or just in a plain bad mood and the likelihood is that your horse will decide to act up. Is it an unfortunate coincidence when this happens? Most unlikely. Develop more awareness of your emotions and acknowledge the effect they have on your horse, not just for your own sake but for your horse's as well.

'But I can't help how I feel,' you may say. If you aren't responsible for your feelings, who is? Your boss? The weather? The traffic? Poor you – living in a constantly reactive state to whatever goes on around you and unable to take any responsibility for how you manage your anger and irritations; and poor horse that has to be around you at some of these times. Consider this, though. Have you ever been in a blazing argument with someone when the phone rang? Did you pick it up and screech, 'What?' at the unsuspecting person on the other end, or were you able to be polite? Perhaps you couldn't contain your emotion and had to say, 'I can't talk now.' Maybe that broke the tension and you were able to return to your argument with an apology and a willingness to listen. If you find that nothing stops that torrent of rage and anger, I suggest that walking away from the situation is your best option. If you find that you can be

> 'I can tell you that while there's not one person in the audience tonight who hasn't heard of me, seen me on television or read something about me, I can also guarantee that not one horse that comes in tonight will have ever heard of me, seen me on television or read anything about me.'
>
> **Monty Roberts at a demonstration**

brought out of feeling angry by a sudden distraction, perhaps you can work on ways to provide that distraction for yourself, or notice when your feelings are escalating and see if you can intercede,

Often people say, 'I love having a horse because it's a way of getting rid of the stress from the rest of my life.' Providing they get rid of the stress with the mucking out and carrying hay that's all right, but not if they carry the stress to their horses. I watched a reality television show recently where a very unhappy young woman was insistently whining that she wanted to go out riding. The owner of the horses explained that it was too hot for the animals to go out at midday but Miss Whiney carried on, 'But I really need to go now because then I can let all my anger out on the horse.' She said it on national television as if this was a perfectly normal, reasonable thing to do.

So you may find that you need some transition time between getting out of your car and getting on your horse. Physical activity is known to elevate mood and, if you need to, you can get angry with a wheelbarrow while mucking out without causing too much distress. However, it's worth taking the time to work out how to enter a positive mental state more quickly. You might even be able to get it down to a few deep breaths and a couple of shoulder shrugs.

Above: 'In the midst of winter, I finally learned that there was in me an invincible summer.'
Albert Camus

Internal dialogue

In order to explore your emotional state, a good question to ask yourself is 'What are you saying to yourself' or 'What did you say to yourself when a certain thing happened?' Could it be relevant to what happened?

While it's unwise to block important emotions that need to be acknowledged and confronted, it's still quite possible to take charge of your mood. Deciding how to manage various situations is often enough. Many irritations can be avoided by thinking ahead and dealing with things as they are and not how they 'should' be. Putting a different label on what's happening is one technique, so that you're not 'stuck in a bloody traffic jam' but 'taking time out to listen to the radio and think in the car'. This change in attitude not only improves your life and blood pressure, but also those of your horse.

Would you like your horse to feel like you do?
How you live your life should reflect your priorities. Put yourself at the top of the list. You're no help to your family, friends, partner – equine or otherwise – if you're constantly stressed, exhausted and/or feeling like you're on a fast-running treadmill. If your horse is going to mirror you, make sure he's reflecting your happiness and calm.

Horses will mirror you physically as well. I'm not thinking of 'the horse that looks most like his owner' competitions, but if you have a back problem or any challenges with your physical alignment, your horse is going to have the same problems because he has to adjust to

---

In an ideal world – how would things be?

What is the quality that some people have that attracts horses, so horses just seem to like being with them? Probably of more value to most of us, can it be attained?

I don't have to go back many years to remember what it was like for me to have absolutely no idea of how to be with horses. Don't get me wrong. I'm not saying I know it all now either, but there is no doubt that things have improved. When I think about some of the confusing scenes in which I was involved, it fills me with horror. At one show I was having a really bad time loading my horse. All the emotions and stress that accompany that situation are probably well known to most of us. 'I really need this horse to get in this lorry pretty quickly, because any minute now someone might see that I can't load my horse. I don't want people to know I can't load my horse – I want people to think I'm good with horses,' and so on and so on. 'Oh my God, please go in the lorry, now!' Even non-believers have been known to pray at the bottom of the ramp on occasion.

In this instance I really did need my horse to load quickly, because in all the fuss he'd ripped off the wing mirror and dented the front wing of the extremely expensive-looking jeep parked next to us. I wanted to get out of that field fast, but did my horse take that on board? I don't think so! I'm not surprised now. The more wound up I became, the less likely I was to get a result.

Several helpers and an hour later, the horse decided that perhaps the lorry might be a preferable place to be than among all the confusion outside it, and off I drove, vowing never, ever to get into a similar situation again.

After a few events like this, if you are still seriously considering a life including horses, you really do have to start asking if there is a way forward that is perhaps a tad less stressful. Could it, in fact, be possible that there is a way of communicating with horses that they understand, whereby when you ask them to do something, they understand what you want and are happy to do it? As I write that last sentence I am thinking of all those thousands of horse people who week in, week out, seem to go about their horse business without ever having to ask questions like this. But that is exactly the thought I used to have all those years ago, when I couldn't get my horse in the lorry, or when I ran him up at the show and he was more interested in mounting the mare in the next-door ring. To this day, I know there are a lot of people who simply cannot see the necessity for exploring the possibility of finding a better way. All I can think is that maybe they aren't starting from the same place I did, or perhaps they simply don't see things the way I do. For me, change had to happen.

For quite a few years of my life, finding a way of being with horses that I am happy with has been on my list of

---

deal with your weight. Whenever you have your horse's back checked, get your own back checked as well. I felt that massages were a little, shall we say, self-indulgent until Pie's masseur pointed out that we'd never get his back right until we got me straightened out.

It's well known that our thoughts affect what's happening in our bodies. That's how lie detector tests work, by testing how your body reacts to your thoughts. Your heart rate, blood pressure, breathing rate, muscle tension and even changes in your temperature can often be detected if you're lying. Negative thoughts physically weaken you by depressing your immune system, as well as making you uptight. Positive thoughts come through in every cell of your body to bring you the positive results you want. Try it next time you go to pick up a bale of hay. Before you pick it up, think about something you're useless at, remember yourself failing, tell yourself that things are awful and you'll

---

major projects. I am pleased with what I have achieved so far – all the more sweet as I have not previously been well known for my long-term dedication to much at all. Originally, I thought that just one or two little tricks would make the difference. Now I am certain that it takes a lot of hard work, lots of experience and a quiet determination to succeed. When I work with other people and their horses, I can see that definitely the most successful are those who take a long-term view, day by day gently working on improving how they are with their horses. I don't want to get too mystical here, but being with a horse and knowing it is relaxing in your company is a deeply satisfying experience that is quite hard to describe in words. Have you heard that saying 'You get what you settle for'? Well, with horses and learning to be a better horseman (and possibly a lot of other things in life, too) it is particularly appropriate – don't settle for confusion and don't settle for just getting by.

If you work on developing a consistent approach to your horsemanship through understanding how the horse's mind works, the horse will appreciate it. You can do it by studying the horse's responses to your actions, and by watching good trainers at work. I once heard two people arguing about horsemanship. One was saying that because we are human we could not hope to communicate with horses in a language that the horse understood. We would make so many mistakes that we shouldn't even try. The other was saying that if you make the effort to communicate, even if you get 50 per cent of it wrong, the horse will know that at least you are trying and will thank you for that. I agree with the second person – horses do pick up on your intent, they do know if you are trying to help them, and if you can show them that, it can be quite surprising how easy the job often turns out to be.

As for how to be with horses and what I have learnt so far, that is not so easy to put into words. My search began by trying this technique and trying that technique, but as time has gone by it has become more a search for a way of being. Now when I look at good horsemen I can see that one of the reasons they are good is because a lot of the time they do very little, but when they do do something it is consistent, fair and the horse understands. They have found a way of being that horses trust – it works for them and it works for the horse.

By the way, I know leaving the damaged jeep was bad karma – I just couldn't deal with it at the time. I hope that it will all come out in the wash in due course.

Recommended Associate Tom Widdicombe

Uncontrollable temper

A client of mine had a lot of difficulty controlling her temper. The first time I met her she had just ridden a horse that had cuts on his side from her spurs. She asked me to work with her nappy horse and things were going very well. He was getting much more confident. So much so that she started to push things too far. When the horse baulked, she got really cross but decided to walk away from the situation to see if she could calm down. She sat down for a while and had a cigarette. 'But it was no good,' she told me. 'I just couldn't help myself. I walked up to the horse and stubbed my cigarette out on him.' What could I say? I managed to persuade her that she wasn't the person to work with this horse and that he should come to me for some more schooling and I'd arrange for him to be re-homed.

Recommended Associate (anonymous to respect client confidentiality)

never pick up this bale. Now heave! Then remind yourself of how strong and capable you are, think of a time when you felt really good and tell yourself you're the best. Feel the power surge through your body. Now lift that bale!

Horses are horses; frustration is usually with ourselves

When it comes to getting upset and frustrated with your horse, stop and think, 'How intelligent is this? What is my horse doing that is so bad?' I'd like to take a guess – he's not behaving like a horse again is he, by any chance? Not standing still at convenient times for the owner? Getting excited when he sees other horses? Unforgivable! These are things that horses do unless their owners have helped them learn that there is a better way to behave. Any time you find yourself becoming unreasonable with a horse – or a child – for behaving, quite naturally, like a horse or a child, look at yourself honestly and work out where you are not happy with your life. Often it's not the horse or child at fault at all – if you feel frustration, then make sure it's only directed at yourself.

Fake it until you make it

Some aspects of competition and giving demonstrations can be useful in more general horsemanship. For one thing, you have to learn to control your emotions. True, it's not unknown for someone to come out of the ring crying and screaming, 'That is SO unfair. I've not got a rosette and if this stupid creature ever canters on the wrong leg again he's dog meat!' but they are generally under nine years old, and improve remarkably by the time they reach ten or eleven.

All the people I work with nowadays are calm and patient around horses. In fact, some of them have reported that when they do see someone screaming at a horse, which they might do at a horse show or in a strange yard, it seems really bizarre, like watching some poor mad person. It's human nature to think that whatever environment you're in is 'normal'. An enormous advantage in having had Monty Roberts as a role model is that I've watched him react to 'disasters' by saying, 'Now how are we going to get this training situation to work out?' Much of my previous experience of watching people with horses in these circumstances was to witness pure fury and frustration. Watching someone with a quiet, thoughtful approach was something of a revolution. In my early days with horses I was encouraged to believe that you were meant to get upset if something didn't go to plan because otherwise people would think (you were always strongly encouraged to worry what 'people would think') you didn't really care, or were incompetent. We put enormous pressure on ourselves when we worry about what 'people might think'. People watching make us embarrassed or self-conscious and so instead of behaving better, we behave worse. Aren't people strange? I suggest you worry less about what people might think and more about what your horse thinks.

It's a common reaction to hold your breath when tense, so remind yourself to breathe, which encourages the horse to breathe as well. To relax, breathe out slowly. As I've become more body aware (thank you, Pilates!) I've become conscious of how my shoulders end up around my ears if I get at all tense. If this is the case with you, deliberately feel your shoulder blades and consciously push them down and give a big sigh, as in, 'My goodness isn't this boring?' Horses will not only mirror but downright mimic at times and your horse is very likely to sigh as well. This is a good sign when you are working together and is often followed by a period when the horse is open to much greater learning.

> 'It's a funny thing about life. If you refuse to accept anything but the best, you very often get it.'
>
> W. Somerset Maugham

Contingency plans

I advise working with a young horse in a round pen or some smallish, enclosed area. Before you start any tasks or actions, do some sort of risk assessment, especially if you have a young horse that bucks or bolts, and imagine a worst case scenario. Ask yourself, 'Do I really feel comfortable doing this?' It doesn't matter if you're entering the Open showjumping that day or picking out your Shetland pony's feet, if the answer's no, carry on by asking yourself, 'What would make me feel safe and comfortable?' The answer might be, 'If the weather was better,' 'If I was in a more suitable arena,' 'If those particular people weren't around right now,' or it might even be, 'I'd really like someone

Opposite: 'There's no secret
so close as that between a
rider and his horse.'
R.S. Surtees, Mr Sponge's
Sporting Tour *(1853)*

more experienced to go through this with me.' The important thing is to realize that everyone needs some help at some time in their lives. If you ever get the feeling of not being able to cope, of not knowing what on Earth you should be doing, it doesn't mean there's anything wrong with you. In fact, congratulate yourself; it simply means you're intelligent enough to think things through.

You can encourage your horse to see you as someone worthy of respect just by the way you move him around. Think about the herd for

CASE STUDY

What horses can teach us about ourselves

Horses were always my sanctuary. I had bought Crystal at a very turbulent time in my life, when lots of changes were occurring and life was somewhat chaotic. I used to go to the yard to sit on an upturned bucket in her stable and listen to her chew her hay. Listening to the rhythmic sound of her munching away enabled me to find a peaceful place at the end of the day. In terms of her schooling, we were doing very gentle groundwork as she was still a young, unstarted horse. Our progress, as is so often the case, had its ups and downs. However, I was constantly a little frustrated that she remained aloof and didn't seem to want to bond with me. Still, I had been warned that this could be a breed characteristic (Lipizzaner x Arab). 'She's a royal lady, my dear,' said the breeder.

Things came to a head one day when I decided to go to the yard to see Crystal after a particularly stressful day at work. As I charged around with all my adrenalin pumping, I was surprised to find Crystal alternating between being totally resistant to what I was trying to achieve and almost aggressive towards me. Then, this little voice popped into my head, 'Your horse is your mirror!' I looked at Crystal and saw myself as she was seeing me – someone who was totally overstressed, swinging between aggression and defensiveness and having a real problem remaining focused and consistent. In her ego-less desire to synchronize with me, she was showing me exactly how I was behaving to others and was mirroring my own emotional turbulence perfectly. What an insight! What a gift from her!

This marked the beginning of a very painful period for me. I gave up my job, which was causing me so much heartache and threatening my mental and physical health. I spent several months severely

contemplating what had brought me to that point, examining what was important to me and what were my deepest personal values. I became depressed and had treatment for chronic anxiety attacks. Crystal again became my sanctuary, providing me with a quiet place to think and a steady presence. She responded faithfully to the changes I made as a person, giving me a yardstick by which I could see my progress out of my own chaos. She provided me with a focus for my dreams as well as something to structure my day around. Going to see Crystal meant that I got out of the house and did something constructive on a daily basis.

As a direct result of these events, we decided as a family to move to France and change our way of life. Of course, Crystal came with us. I decided to do nothing with my horses except get to know them as individuals, as we now had the horses at home. I put all the stress aside and tried to learn how to be with my horses while putting my ego on one side. I had to learn the value of patience and how to be flexible, rather than go all out on one way of doing things and then beat myself in frustration at every barrier that came along. As I rebuilt my own way of doing things, somehow along the way I finally achieved what I had longed for with Crystal. She started to like being around me.

My horse, my friend, helped to save my health, my career, my marriage and my relationship with my children, then happily helped me rebuild my confidence to start a new life in France and my own business. Now, when she asks for a special tail scratch, the kind only humans can do, I feel humbled to oblige.

Wendy Barrellon-Kendell

a moment. The only way one horse can show leadership over another is to move the other horse around. If you can do the same, your horse is going to look at you in a new light. The lead mare leads from the front, so think about your positioning when you lead your horse and don't let him lead you. The stallion drives from behind and perhaps this is why long reining can be so effective for improving a horse's attitude to what he is being asked to do.

Then you can inspire your horse with your confidence even if you're not feeling too sure of yourself. Just act as though you are someone fantastic. Think of *Stars in their Eyes*: 'Tonight, I'm going to be... John Whittaker!'

When we are calm and relaxed around our horses it is rewarding for them to be near us but when we are brittle and upset it is literally repulsive and unpleasant to be near us. Horses pick up on human emotions strongly, tending to match or synchronize with them. If your breathing is hard and shallow, your pulse rate will go up and your horse's is likely to follow suit.

Once you have control of your emotions you can use them to help in the handling and training of your horse. Say you have to load a reluctant horse into a horsebox. It might make sense to act a little irritably when the horse is not focusing on where you want him to go – note I said 'act'. It wouldn't make any sense at all to be irritated. Then as soon as the horse even 'thinks' forward you can instantly soften your attitude, relax, breathe, stroke him, let him feel the benefits of being in a comfortable space with the relaxed you. I have students who, while working well with pressure and release techniques, take a quantum leap forward when they develop this ability to take charge of their emotions. It can be the 'missing link' in their relationship with the horse.

Above: 'What lies behind us and what lies before us are tiny matters compared to what lies within us.'
Oliver Wendell Holmes

Would you say you're a laid-back person, relaxing to be around? Or are you a buzzy person, energising to be around? Now go and ask three honest friends for their opinions. Ask them, if you were a horse, what would you be like? Knowing yourself helps you to understand the reactions you are getting from horses and enables you to enhance or modify your qualities to get the very best results.

Key points

- In the herd, horses have a natural tendency to synchronize with other horses and will do the same with humans.
- Horses love a leader – not a bully but someone who inspires trust and confidence in them.
- Your intention and how you focus your energy affects your horse strongly.
- Day-to-day emotions have a strong effect on work with horses.
- If you have unresolved emotional difficulties, make a decision to handle your emotions in an acceptable way until you feel better.
- Horses will often mirror your pulse rate and emotions, sometimes even how you feel about yourself.
- Value yourself as well as others – nobody loves a martyr, not even your horse.
- If you are new to horses, don't buy a young horse but choose one that is older and more experienced.
- Horses can be our greatest teachers – but only if we are willing to learn from them.

Above: 'Ask me to show you poetry in motion and I will show you a horse.'

Anon

Please ride properly!

As we move on to more adventurous territory – jumping ditches, walking past pigs, riding through water – it's a concern to me to know that none of my brilliant suggestions for calm mental focus, positive visualizations and so on are likely to work if you can't actually ride. Perhaps that's overly harsh – it may be fairer to say, 'if there are important parts of your riding that aren't as effective as they could be'. Perhaps the chapter title should be 'Please evaluate your riding honestly', but I love the expression 'Please ride properly!' and I'll explain why later in the chapter.

Sometimes people guiltily confess that they feel nervous when they are riding and you only have to watch them for a short while to start feeling nervous as well. They are perched precariously on top of a large, unpredictable animal and are clearly unsafe. For the Intelligent Horsemanship Recommended Associates it can be awkward when someone complains about their horse being, say, lazy or flighty, and the RA goes to watch the person ride. The rider's full weight may be slumped on to the back of the saddle and she may be hanging on to the horse's head with hands that have the sensitivity of a rhino wearing mittens. Worst of all, she thinks this is completely normal. In a case such as this, it is

Opposite: 'In riding a horse we borrow freedom.'
Anon

'[Horses] have always understood a great deal more than they let on.
It is difficult to be sat on all day, every day, by some other creature, without forming an opinion about them. On the other hand, it is perfectly possible to sit all day, every day, on top of another creature and not have the slightest thought about them whatsoever.'

Douglas Adams, *Dirk Gently's Holistic Detective Agency*

barely relevant to be looking at the horse at all. The rider has to be encouraged to look at her role in any problems that exist.

This is not to say that you have to be a perfect rider to get results, but you do have to ride well enough to give your horse a chance to get things right. As you step up in confidence and ambition, you need to work harder to improve. For example, my weak lower leg may not be a problem when I take a quiet hack around the lanes but it would be a major disadvantage if I were riding around Badminton, and I'd soon be caught out.

Please note that I'm working on the premise that the likelihood of someone telling you the truth about your inadequate riding is about as high as someone telling you your body odour needs attention. Nobody wants to hurt your feelings – and if some people were told honestly they would be very upset. All their friends would rally round, telling them that of course they are wonderful riders/don't have body odour, crossing their fingers behind their backs. So it would all be back to square one anyway.

'How do you get to Tipperary?' 'Ah well, if I were you I wouldn't start from here...'

Where you are starting from and where you want to get to are important points to consider. Have you ever sat on a horse in your life? Have you been riding for 20 years or more? Are you self-taught or have you had lessons regularly from a particular school of horsemanship? Defining 'riding well' is important, too. Is it to stay on the horse whatever he does, as in the case of a great rodeo rider? Is it to ride the horse from A to B safely, effectively and with consideration, which is a necessary requirement for an endurance rider? Is it to win at polo, racing, eventing, showjumping or at dressage competitions? Think about what you are trying to achieve with your riding. Is it just to feel more secure and safe, or do you have loftier ambitions?

My advice is not to put your friends in the embarrassing situation of saying whether or not they think you can ride well enough for whatever it is you want to do. We have someone who is perfectly capable of making this judgement. (That person is you, incidentally!)

Fitness

In one of Channel 4's *Faking It* programmes, a woman who had never ridden before had to pass herself off as an experienced showjumper. The producers didn't trawl round people's living rooms, pull someone up from their TV dinner and try to turn a couch potato into a horsewoman within four weeks. No, they went out and found 24-year-old Shelley, who was a pole dancer at that time. Although my knowledge of pole dancing is somewhat limited, you only have to try a few of the moves with your pitchfork to realize you have to be fit – particularly in your legs – and have what is often described as 'core stability'.

Left: Practising core stability – 'Without discipline, there's no life at all.'

Katherine Hepburn

Here are some questions to ask as you start to assess if you are the rider your horse deserves or not.

- Can you walk/trot/canter without holding on to anything – including the reins?
- Can you perform five consecutive steps of leg yield/turn about the forehand?
- Can you back up without resistance? Examples of resistance are head in air, mouth open, sideways steps (the horse, that is).
- Have you taught your horse to do simple things, including standing still?
- Do you feel reasonably safe?

I've heard people say 'There are no set rules to riding,' and 'Each person has their own style.' I do agree that the aids can be given in different ways – Western and English weight aids are the complete opposite in some cases – and the different methods used in various disciplines can be equally successful. However, let's look at it from the horse's perspective. It seems likely that, given the choice, a horse would ask to be ridden with the least amount of force or pressure necessary to

> 'It must be weird getting on a horse like, coz it's not like a skateboard when you can just get on and tell it what to do. You have to sort of ask it and stuff and hope they do what you say.'
>
> **Emily's cousin's boyfriend**

provide complete clarity. That's another way of saying he doesn't need to be shouted at but the signals must be clear and consistent enough for him to understand without straining. There are those who believe we could never get our signals so subtle that horses had to strain to hear them, and they could be right! To be considered a decent rider, and therefore fair on your horse, I suggest that, at the very least, you need to be:

- in alignment, i.e. not tipping or falling over to one side or the other, or backwards or forwards;
- stable, so you're not giving aids without realizing it as your legs and arms move;
- aware of your body, so you notice any lack of stability and detect when you are giving aids;
- able to control your movements so you can give precise signals;
- able to receive signals and feedback from your horse;
- able to detect some elements of cause and effect, i.e. know how what you're doing is affecting the horse, and how what he's doing is affecting you. Do you tip forward because he breaks out of canter and into trot, or did he break into trot because you leant forwards?
- willing to adapt what you're doing to suit your horse, but provide enough consistency to avoid the horse becoming confused.

This is all very well – but how do you achieve it?

Core stability

Core stability is vital for more advanced riding, whichever system of riding you adopt, because you want to create a firm foundation for co-ordinated but very minor movements of the legs and arms. It's essential for when the time comes that you want to give the most subtle signals to your horse from movements in the saddle, rather than giving him a kick in the ribs for 'faster' (where you fall back when

Below: Take every opportunity to increase your core stability.

he goes faster) and a pull in the mouth for 'slower' (where you tip forward when he slows).

What is core stability?

Muscles attached to the spine and pelvis and those supporting the scapula (shoulder blades) stabilise the trunk. Abdominal muscles are the main focus of attention as they act like a corset, taking the pressure off the back and pulling other muscles into place. Strong abdominal muscles, particularly those creating the abdominal wall, are considered essential in preventing back injury and ensuring optimal performance in physical activity.

A good way to feel where they are is to have a big laugh. The corset muscles are those that contract as you bellow. They include the muscles of your 'six pack' (it's there, even if you can't see it) and the muscles that run up and down your back.

Get to work!

Exercises are much more fun if there's a group of you working together. A synergy comes into play and everyone improves much more than an individual would on her own. Your group can be just two, which is pretty small, or up to perhaps eight people.

1 Go to the gym. The fitness industry is recognizing the benefits of developing 'core strength' for all forms of physical activity. Core training sets out to improve posture and body alignment, the importance of which has long been a key component of Pilates, yoga and t'ai chi. These are great ways to start developing core stability.

Above: 'We cannot guarantee success but we can deserve it.'
George Washington

2 Book a lesson on the lunge. Someone else controls the horse from the middle and you don't have to think about steering or paces at all. You are there to concentrate on feel and your position. Discuss with the instructor how far you can progress. Tie the reins up and do windmills and other exercises with your arms. Vary the direction of your gaze. Later, take your stirrups away and see if you can balance and feel in harmony in just the same way at different paces. If you are anxious and slide all over the place, do not pass

- If a horse is not fully fit and pain free, he will be unable to respond to the best of his ability and it may result in signals getting mixed for him.
- There is no point in getting your horse 'fixed' physically if you don't get yourself done at the same time – treat yourself as well for your horse's sake! If your back is out and you are lopsided, you are going to keep putting your horse's back out and he's going to have to make constant adjustments to carry you. It's so important for a rider to stay supple and body-aware. For instance, can you touch your toes? Can you look equally far over both shoulders? For how long can you hold a riding position?
- While riding, communication with the horse is mainly via a series of tiny signals. If you don't have an independent seat, you have no base from which to give these signals.
- If you're not fully in control of your body movements, you will confuse the messages to the horse, adding to his stress. Horses can feel the most subtle body movements – even the rider's breathing – through the saddle and saddle pad.

go (or collect £200!) but invest in more lunge lessons until you start to feel secure and confident.

3 Ride with just a bareback pad during a lesson on the lunge.

4 Watch really good, effective riders – keep how they appear on a horse in your mind's eye (imagine how they might be thinking and feeling as well). If there are no suitable riders around then buy or hire a video of a rider you admire and really study. Beg, borrow (but don't steal) a video camera. Get a friend (or better still a member of your group) to video you (or use the film option on a digital camera – these can be downloaded very easily and quickly onto a computer) when riding, at a walk, at a trot, at a canter (if appropriate), from directly behind, from directly in front, from the side. Preferably have fairly slimline clothing on. Watch the results with your friend or the group. What's the most obvious difference between you and the top riders? Are you sitting up reasonably straight in the saddle, not hollow-backed, just supporting yourself? Do you look fairly stable? Or are you flopping around? Do you look like you could fall

Tip for tippers: When you are driving a car and you have to stop suddenly, do you flop forwards? Unlikely, because you are aware what is going to happen so you anticipate and tighten the appropriate muscles in the thighs and abdomen to keep you upright. Apply this method when you're riding.

backwards or forwards at any moment? Are you lopsided? Where does it look like your weight is in the saddle? Are you supporting your weight evenly or is your backside pressing all your weight at the back of the saddle, making it uncomfortable for your horse?

5 Invent your own dressage test – you can even decide where the letters are positioned. Practise a little and then see how well you can perform it. Can you get your horse to trot, canter on the right leg and halt, all at specific points? Include some leg yielding – not to be fancy but for practical reasons. The fact is, if you can't get your horse to move away from your leg at any given time, strictly speaking you and your horse are not safe to be going on the roads, particularly if a car comes alongside you too fast and you can't squeeze to the side.

Below: Christopher Bartle coaching Bettina Hoy at the World Equestrian Games, Jerez 2002.

Good riders keep having lessons

It's a fact that the really good riders, including those of Olympic standard, continue to have lessons and take advice right through their careers. I was talking with a colleague the other day and he told me how he learned a lesson about people who describe themselves as 'very good riders'. He started a young horse for the owner, who was looking forward to riding the horse himself, and kept saying, 'I'm a very good rider, you know.' His girlfriend repeated it later – 'He's a very good rider, you know.' When the day came for the owner to ride his horse, my friend gave him a leg up and the owner said, 'I'm a very good rider, you know – I've been on a horse four times!'

Good horse people keep schooling their horses. Many people aim to keep a horse at the same standard without trying to improve his way of going. Often the horse will start to resist and problems may occur simply because he isn't supple enough to do what is asked.

6 Video someone else riding your horse and see how he goes for her. Compare notes. Does she feel he's resistant to the right or doesn't answer to the leg? If you are in a group, this is an opportunity for you to be filmed riding someone else's horse to see what the differences and similarities are to riding your own.

7 Video your horse naked (that is without anyone on his back) and see how his movement compares to when he's being ridden.

8 Try this co-ordination exercise when sitting on a chair, lying in bed or riding your horse – just don't try it when driving! Rotate one arm backwards (or rotate one hand clockwise if lying in bed). Then circle your foot in the same direction. Now change the direction in which you circle your foot while keeping your arm/wrist rotating smoothly in the same direction as before. Easy? Responses range from finding it downright impossible to being able to do it but losing fluency and smoothness. If you find it really difficult, break it down into smaller parts. Move your foot a quarter turn to the left at the same time as moving your hand a quarter turn to the right. Make your movements small so you don't get tired out. Keep trying. If you find it easy, concentrate on smoothness, and then try more complicated co-ordinations. Use opposite hands and feet. Use both arms and legs. Circle your right hand and right foot in the same direction, and your left hand and left foot in opposite directions. Then swap. Check – or ask someone else to check – that you are doing it properly. If you're finding it easy, you've either got amazing neurological wiring or you're cheating!

The reality gap

An example of the difference between what people say and the reality of the situation is provided by my friends and Recommended Associates Lin and Sylvia Whitehouse, both experienced horsewomen. Lin was Hickstead All England Junior Champion on her top pony Grey Fury and Sylvia also competed successfully, including being placed at Hickstead in Open classes. Sylvia and Lin went for a holiday in the Caribbean and were unable to resist an opportunity to ride horses on the beach. First of all they had to fill in a questionnaire. On it they were asked if they considered themselves to be 'novice riders', 'good riders' or 'excellent riders'. They both ticked 'good riders'. It turned out everyone else had put themselves down as 'excellent riders' and so Lin and Sylvia were the only ones in the group who weren't allowed to canter along the beach!

What's the purpose of the exercises?

Well, if you can't perform these movements, it seems unlikely that you'll be able to apply aids independently of each other. Is it possible that every time you kick you might accidentally pull with your hands at the same time? Perhaps your left foot joins in all the time? Doing exercises comprising non-habitual movements improves your co-ordination.

Once you're reasonably proficient at them, ask someone to call instructions for you. Don't try it before then as you'll both fall about laughing at your early attempts! Responding to your friend's calls will improve your ability to interpret and respond to instructions while simultaneously taking several other things into account. This is known as parallel processing in scientific terminology. Riding well requires huge ability in the parallel-processing department. You need to know what you're doing with your body and what the horse is doing with his while keeping in mind the vision you're working towards. At the same time you must evaluate the difference between ideal state and current state and work out how to get from one to the other, and notice that since you thought that last thought everything has changed. You have to be able to respond instantaneously and con-tinuously while indicating to the horse where you would like him to go and listening to instructions from your teacher, perhaps having to avoid other riders, or the walls. No wonder it's not as simple as 'sit up straight, heels down, now piaffe!' By the time you acquire all these skills and become a competent rider, you'll have what it takes to be a good fighter pilot – or at least to do well on computer games.

It's not within the scope of this book to give you all the technical information on riding. It can be very heavy going reading about 'your hip bone connected to your thigh bone and your thigh bone connected to your knee bone', and people's opinions vary so much, but there are some excellent riding books on the market (see Website). If you are following a class with a specific teacher or one of her disciples – Mary Wanless, Sylvia Loch or Sally Swift, for instance – it's a good idea to have that teacher's book so that you can keep checking the instruction you're receiving to ensure you're understanding it correctly.

Choosing your instructor

If your horse is not responding as you wish, consider what you need to do differently: enlisting the help of the right instructor can make an enor-mous difference. There are many excellent instructors but that doesn't

Being aware of personal fitness

'It's also necessary to have instructors who are aware of one's body shape/conformation and personal fitness. My mother, who is just learning to ride at 63 and has some of the stiffness and lack of suppleness you can associate with being 63, had as an instructor a young girl who made her trot for 30 minutes with no stirrups. Despite my mother telling the instructor that she wasn't up to this and it was really too much, the instructor insisted she carried on until my mother had to stop the lesson in tears because it hurt so much.'

Intelligent Horsemanship student
Alex Jacob-Whitworth

'Learn all the technical stuff and then forget it, just play!'

Charlie Parker

necessarily make them excellent for you. You need to know yourself well before making a decision. Some people don't mind being shouted at aggressively, whereas others hate it. Some people prefer plenty of theory before being asked to do anything, others just want action.

Personal recommendation is fine but remember that the instructor has got to suit your situation as well as your personality, e.g. distance, money, times available, so be prepared to shop around until you find the right person. It's a good idea to watch an instructor giving a lesson before making the final decision. Never book a course of lessons without having an assessment lesson first. I once made this mistake, booking my first course of massage treatments – it was pure hell. The lady never stopped telling me her business problems and asking me what she should do. I was invariably more stressed coming out than when I went in. Ask questions on the phone beforehand. Don't wait until the day of the lesson to see if an instructor agrees with your standards and values.

Be straightforward with the potential instructor at this stage to avoid misunderstanding. For instance, if you're nervous, say so. If you don't wish to carry a whip or spurs, say so, too. If you have had a bad experience with another instructor, you will know the particular situations you want to avoid. It helps the instructor to understand what you need and he or she may even feel it's best to recommend someone else, who would be better suited to you.

Look out for...

THE CHARMER

It's quite possible to find a totally charming and delightful instructor whom you would like to have as your best friend but who doesn't assist your riding in any way whatsoever. I spotted these when I went to watch my niece Daisy have some lessons. The 'babysitter', or perhaps 'paid friend', is wonderful company and possibly an excellent rider herself but does little more than give instructions on direction or pace for 40 minutes, accompanied with a constant barrage of 'Lower leg back a little', 'Lovely!', 'Shoulders back', 'Soooooper!' If she keeps up a good pace, the rider will feel relieved it's not a full hour. A question I asked myself at the end of one of these lessons (and perhaps I wouldn't have asked it if the lesson had been around £20 rather than £65) was if Daisy had a lesson once a week for the next year (£3,510), would she be any the wiser? Would she be able to start teaching herself because she had learned so much? Come to think of it, would she have learned anything at all except how to listen to and follow instructions obediently? The answer I came up with was 'extremely doubtful'.

The Motivator

Motivators can definitely play a part in improving your riding (and, indeed, your life at appropriate times). To have an experienced person who knows what she's talking about putting up the jump and saying, 'You can do it!' is an excellent idea. Perhaps you're more scared of disappointing them than you are of the jump so you surpass yourself. Fantastic! I just want you to ask yourself whether you're finding good answers to any questions you may have and whether this instructor may be more suitable as an occasional teacher than full time. Can you and your horse keep up the improvements you've made when you get home? The eventual aim is to be able to motivate yourself.

Here again, working within a support group can be motivating in itself. As I'm getting back into jumping after more than 20 years, I have loved the few lessons I've managed to fit in with Pat Burgess. Pat trained Richard Meade, Lucinda Prior-Palmer (now Green) and Virginia Holgate (now Eliot) to great success in the '70s. Her group lessons are more like parties with, say, six riders and their friends all mucking in together to rearrange the grids and jumps and organizing the tea and cakes. The horses are very relaxed with the stopping and starting while everyone takes their turn to jump. I wouldn't want to swap a group lesson with Pat for an individual one. You learn so much more within the group because you're watching the other riders and hearing what she's saying to them. One of my biggest weaknesses is a tendency for my lower leg to move back when Pie jumps. Pat spotted this straight away, of course, reminding me 'to keep that lower leg forward' and conjuring up some wonderful mind pictures, such as 'imagine you're going to kick him in the jaw as he jumps!' What probably helped as much, though, was that in the same lesson I had the opportunity to watch 'Miss Tenth at Badminton with Perfect Lower Leg'. I kept a picture of her jumping action in my mind and, for me, that really helped me. I believe it's the same with the Intelligent Horsemanship foundation courses. Within a friendly group atmosphere, people of quite varying standards learn almost by osmosis, everyone tending to rise on the same tide.

> 'Don't learn the tricks of the trade – learn the trade.'
>
> **Anon**

The Tyrant

Whether you're willing to accept being sworn at, screamed at and humiliated comes down to what you're trying to achieve. If you are merely trying to develop a decent riding position in order to have fun, an instructor who undermines you or makes you feel uncomfortable is inappropriate. However, it's not as simple as saying, 'Don't ever put up with this.' Supposing this instructor happens to be the best in the country and has the knowledge that you want? Having had more than one experience of this, the advice I'd offer is don't take anything personally. Pick out the information you want and take it away with you. After all, it's extremely unlikely that the instructor has a personal grudge against you. People who behave tyrannically were probably taught that way and haven't learned to do it differently, or, let's be generous here, perhaps they are just extremely passionate about their subject.

However, do check that an instructor of this sort does know what he or she is talking about. I've known some abusive instructors who are incompetent and who keep on with their behaviour because it stops anyone questioning them. At 13 years old I wasn't familiar with the idea of not taking things personally. I'd just won a scholarship for promising junior showjumpers with a pony who was fairly new to me. He was nervous and had obviously had a difficult time (i.e. been beaten up) in the past, so was quite erratic, but we were making progress. It was the proudest moment of my life to have achieved this scholarship and the pony and I were both doing our best. However, on the final day of the four-day course, when some parents were invited, the instructor couldn't resist the lure of an audience. He seemed to think that screaming and shouting made him look like a star. He was a man in his 50s – I was just a little girl, for goodness' sake! With the pony not ready for a course of 3ft 9in fences, the more he shouted the more like jelly the pony and I became.

Life can send little kindnesses to help in those bad times – your Guardian Angel can show up in many disguises. Just as all my hopes and dreams were crumbling away forever and I was thinking I wasn't fit to ride a pony at all, never mind round a showjumping course, a little voiced piped up, 'She can ride my pony if she likes.' The instructor looked round with a sneer but this other little girl had already jumped off and was leading her pony towards me. 'Here she can have a go on Bonnie Lass.' I felt even worse now. Here I was, a disaster, and she was giving me her pony to ruin as well! I climbed on to Bonnie Lass in a

'My religion is kindness.'

Dalai Lama

numb, almost catatonic state, which was not ideal, pointed her at the fences and this gorgeous, generous, no-hang-ups pony (just like her owner) popped round the fences with me. Bonnie Lass and her owner, Rosemary Lambden, gave me the strength to hang on in there a bit longer, for which I'll always be grateful.

Life moves in mysterious ways though. A few years later I happened to call in on this instructor's yard. He was on a young horse. I'd never seen him ride before and was shocked at how stiff he looked. He was clearly one of those people who believed that riding was something you 'did' to a horse, there was no impression of partnership and harmony. After we'd spoken, he decided to pop the horse over a tiny jump, it wasn't even a foot high. The horse stopped and he fell off, smack, at my feet. It was at that moment I got my sense of humour back about the whole situation.

> To achieve what you want consistently takes more than hope – it takes planning.

THE GENIUS

Here I'm talking about the person who is performing at the top of their discipline, not someone who has actually set themselves up to be a teacher. The trouble with the genius performer is that very often, every-thing has become so easy for them that he often doesn't actually know what it is he does that makes them so successful. This can be frustrating for them and the student. Even more so if he thinks he knows what his secret of success is, but it's not really the case. The title of this chapter was inspired by watching genius showjumper David Broome teach a clinic; he was watching a girl flounder around with her horse and things clearly weren't working out. Eventually he said in a frustrated, though not unkind, manner, 'Now come on – just ride properly!'

I would highly recommend that you spend as much time around the geniuses as you can, but beware of making false assumptions, such as, 'They smoke forty cigarettes a day, so that must be a good idea' or 'They ride their horses in such-and-such a bit, therefore it must be right.' Sounds ridiculous? Well, when I was a junior showjumper, everyone had their horses in green and white plastic schooling boots because their hero at that time, Alwin Schockemohle, did. And yes, I admit it – I had some too!

However, do try to take in every move they make on a horse, imagine how they must be feeling, breathing, thinking and try to work out for yourself the secrets of their success. By all means ask them questions but don't forget the advice in Chapter 1 about intelligent timing when to ask! Don't necessarily expect precise answers. In fact, the genius who performs very much 'in the zone' (meaning on a mainly subconscious level in this instance) is likely to be completely put off if you ask them, 'How do you see the stride as you come around a sharp bend?' just before they go in the ring. Thinking about it consciously could be enough to wreck their performance!

Coaches
In the corporate world, life coaches are becoming more and more popular, and coaches are regarded as essential for serious sportspeople. Instead of being given repeated instructions and told what to do, with a coach people are expected to become more fully engaged in the process of improving their performances. Once the goal is established the coach should listen, observe and customize his approach to suit individual needs. He must work to keep the client focused and on track to overcome any challenges and obstacles that arise on the way to the goal.

Obviously, some coaches are better than others. The best coaches are knowledgeable in the subject, enabling them to pose relevant questions, but not necessarily as good as you or better. Coaches are mentors who have the experience to show you the shortcuts. They will help you to discover for yourself how to improve. In riding, most people need help from an expert because it can take too long and be too frustrating for both horse and rider to be left to work it out indefinitely. I guess the best riding instructors are a combination of both teacher and coach.

However, don't underestimate the value of questions from people outside the field – that uninformed question about why you seem to have so much pressure on the horse's mouth when you said you were working on lightness, for instance. If ever you find yourself saying, 'Oh, it's too complicated, you wouldn't understand,' just think about it. Perhaps there's a hole in your understanding. If your instructor ever says, 'Well, that's just the way it is,' question her understanding. It's reasonable for someone to say, 'We're not quite at that point yet, and I'm not sure it will make much sense to you until we cover this area,' but if they're not prepared to offer some sort of broad explanation, be a little suspicious.

Working with a coach

First, you have to identify what it is that you want. You have to start with a goal. Then you and your coach can work out a plan of action together on how to achieve it. If you have difficulty in deciding what you do want, think about what you do not want – that's often easier. Chances are that you want the opposite of what you say you don't want.

In order to achieve most goals, it's necessary to break them down into small chunks. Be careful about whom you reveal your important higher goals to. If your coach has little talent or imagination, or is jealous and bitter because he feels life owes him more, you're probably not going to get the most supportive reaction when you say you want to win dressage competitions at grand prix level. In fact, even the most supportive coach may find it hard to keep a straight face if you and your broken-down ex-racehorse come along with no experience or financial support and make a statement like that – even though stranger things have happened. Jane Savoie is a case in point. She was in exactly that position but through hard work and determination she was eventually so successful she went as reserve on the US Olympic team to Barcelona.

Let's go through an imaginary coaching session. The coach will tend to reiterate what you're saying in order to be sure that you are both quite clear.

'What is it you'd like to achieve in these ten sessions we're going to work together?'

'That's fine – you're not really sure but you know you don't want to keep looking like a real incompetent every time you go in for one of the local dressage competitions?'

'I know what you mean. You're only doing it for fun but you think you'd enjoy it more if you and your horse didn't look like you'd met in a bar an hour earlier and were now hopelessly drunk and staggering around lost.'

'I do understand what you mean about trying to make a big joke of it because you're embarrassed. Don't feel alone – lots of people do that.'

'So that's what you don't want. Can you rephrase it so we can see what you do want?'

'Hmm, OK. You would like your horse and you to do a preliminary dressage test in an acceptable fashion without people laughing at you.'

'So how would you judge "an acceptable fashion"?'

'If you got over six marks for each section, would that be acceptable?'

'That would be amazing! Well, that's terrific then!'

'OK, let's look at the preliminary test and see what it is we need to achieve.'

'What do you feel is the first thing that we need to do?'

'That's correct, we need to walk in.'

'What do you see is the problem with that at the moment?'

'Yes, it's going to be difficult while you still keep slipping off the side.'

Teaching your own family

'It's a wonderful thing to be able to impart all your wisdom to your children, ensuring that they will never have to make the mistakes that you made.' Only those who dropped out of family life to watch Hollywood movies around the clock will not have a face that is overcome with incredulity at this point. Sorry, I'll be serious and say instead that there will more than likely be a time in your life when your own children won't want to learn anything from you – probably around the teenage years. Even if you are the leader in the field of your particular sport/career, it is quite possible you will not be able to pass on any helpful tips to them directly. Even Zara Phillips was quoted in the newspapers as saying that she finds it very difficult being taught by her father, Mark Phillips, international rider and Olympic coach, and they constantly get into arguments. It is quite likely you will have to find some other teacher and pay them to tell your child the information you wish them to learn. This keeps money in circulation and so is good for both the economy and, perhaps more importantly, your sanity.

P.S. Note to teenagers. Don't worry too much if your parents are impossible, embarrassing and don't understand you at all right now – they often improve a great deal as you get into your twenties.

Teaching by example

A student of mine was shocked when she saw her three-year-old daughter shouting and hitting her toy horse at home. She realized that she had picked this up from how the other riders at the livery yard she visited treated their horses. It reminded me of how psychologists sometimes watch children with dolls because children often treat dolls in the same way they have been treated. My student found her daughter's behaviour so worrying that she moved livery yards.

On a far more positive note, our Recommended Associate for Cornwall, Dan Wilson, was amazed when he watched his three-year-old daughter, Lauren, leading an old pony around in the haphazard way you would expect a little girl to do. When the pony stopped and refused to go on, without giving it a second thought, Lauren just changed the angle at which she was leading the pony so that he went with her easily. She had never been taught to do this and Dan was amazed at how much she'd obviously been taking in without him being aware of it. I guess we're back to the old adage that the best way to make a difference is by example.

'What would you suggest the first thing we work on should be?'

'Balance! Excellent! I think you're absolutely right. Balance is going to be a great starting point to achieving our goal.'

'Do you think there is anything that would help your balance?'

'Yes, I think you're right again. Those oversized rubber boots really are not helping and we're going to be challenged in this for as long as your arm remains in a sling...' and so on.

Above: 'Every horse and pony deserves at least once in his life to be loved by a little girl.'

Anon

Top tips for teachers

- Teaching is one of the most powerful ways to learn.
- The most important thing your student wants from you is your attention. Switch off mobile phones and politely postpone conversations with friends and visitors until later.
- Students are entitled to a reasonable amount of confidentiality.

If you are ever planning to say something negative about a student to a third party, pause for a moment and think how the student is going to feel when she hears about it, because she probably will (not to mention how you will feel). There's nothing more off-putting than hearing a teacher being negative about his other students because you know he'll be saying horrible things about you next.

- If you don't like or approve of a student, politely explain that you don't feel you're the right person to teach him or her. Otherwise you're taking money under false pretences.
- Be careful of assumptions. Beware of jargon and ask the students whether they understand. Even, or especially, expressions such as 'use more leg' or 'get him on the bit' mean different things to different people or, surprisingly often, are completely meaningless altogether!
- Treat your students as well as you do your horses. If a horse doesn't understand something after a couple of attempts, you find a different way of explaining it to him. The same goes for students: if they don't understand after you've made a point twice, don't assume they're stupid. Rephrase it or bring them into the middle and check they're hearing you correctly. See if you can find another way of explaining it.
- Don't just correct what a student is doing wrong. Remember to catch her doing something right and use praise generously.
- It's not just each student who is individual – each combination is unique as well. Look at the horse and rider together to judge what is going to suit them.
- Remember that when we're learning something new, our bodies don't always automatically obey. Just because your student isn't doing something you've asked, it doesn't necessarily mean she's ignoring you. We often need to practise over and over again before a movement becomes second nature.
- Be sensitive to students. Some people ride a couple of times a week only and are not as fit as others.

CASE STUDY

Instructors are not always right

I discarded an old instructor because she used to tell me all about how rubbish the rider/horse in the previous lesson had been, thus implying that she would discuss my faults with the next rider. When I saw, on a photo, that I had been riding with one leg further forward than the other, she told me, 'You always ride like that.' I wondered why, in my previous five weekly lessons, she had never mentioned it. The final insult was when she told me I should send my mare to the kennels as she would never jump. I changed instructors, learned to jump and was offered a large sum of money for the mare as 'she was a natural showjumping winner'. However, I kept her until she died a natural death.

Catherine Walker

- Metaphors work well for some people, so use your imagination to help students remember important points. For example, 'Imagine your reins are made of cotton and you have to be very careful not to break them. Feel whether you can slow your horse down by just gently making your body still.'
- Remember your student is entitled to know not just what you want her to do but also why you want her to do it in a particular way. It's the student's right to ask questions – sometimes it means you have to think hard but it's a tremendous way for you to learn as well.
- Take lessons yourself from time to time, not necessarily in riding. Aside from continuous personal development, advantages include being reminded what it's like to be a student and how it feels to be a complete novice. It can really improve your teaching.
- Consider going on a course specifically designed to improve your teaching and communication skills.
- Always finish your lesson on a good note.

Key Points

- Be aware that your riding needs improving, however good you think you are. You may even be the reason for your horse's ridden problems.
- Assess your own riding and then set yourself relevant goals to become what you consider to be a better rider.
- Improve your core stability to become a more balanced and co-ordinated rider.
- Complete the exercises in this chapter, and make sure you've done the ones on feel and timing in Chapter 1. They will have a positive effect on your riding, and be good fun, too.
- Be careful to choose an instructor who is right for you.
- Try working with a coach to help you clarify and reach your goals.
- If you are an instructor, remember you need to keep learning new skills and working on your own continuous improvement as well as that of your students.

CASE STUDY

The teacher must teach

Another excellent teacher I had a few years ago used to teach my husband and myself. My husband is a nightmare for a bad teacher and a dream for a good one – he is completely impossible to intimidate, and if he doesn't understand something, he will halt the horse and gaze wearily at the instructor, before witheringly pointing out that he or she hasn't explained properly. This particular instructor absolutely loved teaching my husband. She used to say that he forced her to come out with the most creative and off-the-wall things in order to get him to understand. It was never a problem if he didn't understand the first time. She felt it was her responsibility to keep explaining until he got it. She really believed the saying, 'If the pupil has not learned, the teacher has not taught.'

Cyberkitten (from the IH Discussion Group)

The art and science (and fun) of long lining

Long lining is often described as 'riding from the ground'. It's easy to see why it's useful with young horses as preparation for the first rider, or to prepare a horse for harness. It has some of the advantages of riding, because you can use rein aids and the equivalent of leg aids, but the horse doesn't have the weight of the rider to contend with. It can also be great for bringing a horse slowly back to work after an injury, but what about you and your horse? If you have an established, fit, rideable horse, why is long lining such a useful skill to have in your repertoire?

I hope by the end of this chapter you'll see why, and if you already long line your horse, perhaps you'll pick up some new ideas.

Can't I do all that with lungeing?

Lungeing aficionados might argue that you can achieve the same results with lungeing as with long lining. You can vary the size of the circle, go in straight lines, pop over trotting poles and fences, vary the rhythm and tempo, make transitions and teach voice commands. However, the single line used doesn't replicate riding in any way. The rein and equivalent leg aids are completely absent. Also lateral work is very tricky on a single line, and generally the changes of direction can't be made on the go. The most important reason to avoid lungeing, though, is that by not being able to control your horse's head equally from both sides you have less control and your horse is very likely to start to tip his head outwards on the circle which will also negatively affect his pelvic girdle and hindquarters. This will also encourage him to canter disunited (with the wrong hind leg leading) and cause physical discomfort that could become permanent. These effects are lessened if the horse is wearing side reins, or anything to improve his symmetry,

Opposite: Pie jumping a ditch and tyres on long lines – 'variety is the spice of life!'

but I would advise going straight for two lines – honestly, it's not as difficult as you might think!

When I first thought about putting Pie over a water ditch (as described later in Chapter Six), I thought that lungeing would be easier because I'd have less to hold in my hands – what a mistake! As soon as Pie had jumped the ditch he started flying around, alternatively coming too close or pulling on the line. Voice commands become much less effective once the adrenalin is up and I wasn't able to keep him on the outside of the circle to jump or steady him up without hauling him in or facing him at a wall. It wasn't pretty or enjoyable at all! Compare that to my first experience of long lining Pie over a water ditch (and this was in an open field rather than an indoor school as before) – give me two lines any time!

The uses of long lining

- Introducing young/green/unstarted horse to rein aids.
- Explaining aids to older horse needing re-education.
- Rehabilitating a horse that's had time off, through injury or otherwise.
- Teaching new school movements.
- Dealing with napping.
- Introducing new objects/situations – 'spook busting'.
- Observing the horse's movement, from beside and behind.
- Suppling and building the horse's muscles.
- Improving the horse's balance.
- Improving the horse's movement.
- Warming up horse and rider before riding.
- Settling an exuberant horse before riding.
- Trotting the horse over poles, jumping.
- Exercising a child's pony.
- Fittening the horse – and the long liner!

The list is limited only by your imagination. Traditional great Academies, including the Cadre Noir and the Spanish Riding School, even use long reining to teach lateral movements, piaffe and the 'airs above the ground' (advanced dressage movements where the horse has all four legs off the ground at the same time, e.g. capriole).

Being able to long line adds variety to the activities you already do with your horse. If you currently work your horse, say, five times a week, then as well as hacking out and schooling you could incorporate long lining as well. You may even find that both your ridden work and your relationship with your horse improve as a result.

Imagine the following scenarios:

Doris, Mary and Jill are buddies and keep their horses at the same yard. On Sundays they all spend time with their horses. Usually they ride out or school together but one Sunday, for a variety of reasons, they decide to do something different. How could long lining help them?

Doris came to horses late in life and eventually bought Nobby, a safe, sensible ride and drive cob. Both horse and owner could be described as 'good doers'. Doris would like to get fitter but finds it hard to fit more exercise into her busy schedule. She certainly doesn't want to be at the gym when she could be spending time at the stables, but hacking out and grooming aren't really doing enough to keep her weight down. She decides it would be fun to try long lining.

Now, Nobby has been driven, so he's used to the feeling of lines around his quarters. All the same, Doris is careful not to take any unnecessary risks and decides to introduce the lines carefully in the enclosed area of their small school. She also removes the jumps that had been left up in the middle of the school, because she doesn't want to get tangled up in them, and she wears her hat and gloves and sturdy boots, as she would when she rides. Doris asks Mary, who is experienced with long lining, to watch and be there to help her if she needs it. She decides to use a roller, because that's what Nobby is used to from being driven, and her aim is simply to walk and trot some simple figures – circles, figures of eights, rein back and transitions.

Doris finds it a bit harder than she expected. She hadn't fully appreciated quite how deep the school was, for example, until she found herself jogging up the long side! It took her a while before she could accurately steer Nobby where she wanted him to go, and occasionally found herself in the wrong place and causing him to change direction unexpectedly. She certainly feels like she got her exercise but she was really pleased to be able to watch Nobby move, and noticed that he began to move a lot more freely as he warmed up. She had a lot of fun with all the circles and turns and felt a real sense of achievement in being able to communicate with him in this way. She's contemplating trotting over poles and small fences next.

Now consider Mary. She's just started lateral work under saddle with her dressage horse, Misterposh, but she can't ride him at the moment because she's sent her saddle away to be re-flocked. He's had a lot of time off in the past due to injury and she really wants to do something with him now that he's fit and sound. She's long lined before, it was how she got him back from his injuries, so she decides to have a go at lateral work on the lines.

First of all, she does a little work on the ground to remind him about moving sideways away from pressure, standing beside him and pressing his side with her hand and then standing beside him with the line held in a coil and tapping it against his body. When she's certain that he understands and isn't terrified of the lines, she fixes the line to the Dually or bit to see how he is when working from behind. She asks Doris to be around to help, in case he doesn't quite get the idea and it takes two to make it clearer to him, but she's pleased at how quickly he picks it up. From the ground she can see for the first time how much stiffer he is to the right than the left, and why he finds some movements much harder than others. Without her weight unbalancing him, though, he really begins to get it, and at the end he's much better on his stiffer side than he was at the beginning. She thinks, 'Perhaps if I can get him really good at this without me on his back, he'll find it a lot easier under saddle when I do try it again.'

Jill's horse, Flight, is quite spooky and she's ended up on the floor more than once when he's suddenly whipped around. She's been doing

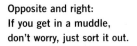

**Opposite and right:
If you get in a muddle,
don't worry, just sort it out.**

some spook-busting work with him, which has been going well. He's happy to go past almost anything so long as she's leading him and walking between him and the scary object. However, although he has become bolder, he's still not happy to be ridden past certain objects. Jill has lost her confidence and tends to tense up when he does. She knows that's not helping. Jill thinks long lining may help them get their confidence back together but she isn't sure she's got enough control. She decides to set up an obstacle course in the school to check and asks Doris and Mary to help in case Flight needs some reassurance, or one of the obstacles needs adjusting.

When Flight whips around, Jill has to be especially quick-witted to prevent him from getting tangled in the lines. He really doesn't want to walk past Mary with the umbrella, nor over the tarpaulin, and it takes a while before he's brave enough to do either. Jill has a real sense of achievement when he finally does both, and is more confident about her chances of doing it under saddle. However, she is glad to be long lining in a small school first, and decides she won't be going out and about on lines until they've both really got the hang of it. In the meantime, there are a multitude of scary objects she can include in her spook-busting, and once she's done the course on lines a few times, and Flight is calm about it, she's sure she'll be happy to ride it, too.

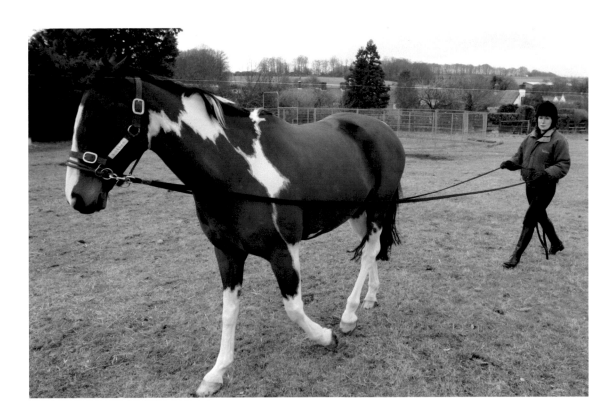

Above: Pie long lining in a Dually. He looks a bit like a donkey here, but that's because he's thinking about what I'm asking.

Equipment

The equipment you need depends on the type of long lining you intend to do. In its simplest form, all you need is a headcollar or Dually halter and two lines. If you use your normal riding tack, you could just use a spare stirrup leather or strap to tie the stirrups together under the horse's body. We usually call this strap a 'hobble'. You can even run the stirrups up and pass the long lines through them. Alternatively, you can use a roller with rings or even turrets. There are advantages and disadvantages to each approach and the choice will depend on individual circumstances.

Headcollar or Dually halter and two lines
This is an excellent choice in the winter. Your horse is caked from head to toe in mud and you have half an hour to work with him. You estimate it would take at least 45 minutes to clear enough mud for saddle and bridle patches but you were so looking forward to doing something constructive with him. Long lining straight off the headcollar or Dually means you can spend zero time scraping mud and maximum time exercising. The advantages of having a dually for long lining are that you

can fit it more snugly to your horse's head to avoid it slipping and it has the two custom made side rings.

This is also possibly the safest way of introducing lines to the horse for the first time (see below).

(see below)

Above: Pie long lining in full tack – 'all dressed up and ready to go!'

Plus points:
- Minimal tacking up is required.
- Inside line goes directly to the Dually, so there's no backward pull and an open rein is possible.
- Lines are unlikely to get tangled.
- Lines are much easier to remove if they lie straight over the horse's back, rather than around the quarters.

Minus points:
- Lines are harder to control and have a tendency to flip up over the horse's back, so they are no longer around the quarters, particularly in changes of direction.
- Very careful attention is required to ensure lines don't drop to the floor.

Stirrups down fixed together under horse's stomach with hobble
This is a great option if you're long lining as a warming up exercise, for both you and your horse, prior to riding, or to get rid of excess energy if your horse is a bit fizzy. You're already tacked up anyway, so adding the stirrup hobble is no hassle.

Plus points:
- Lines are easier to handle and less likely to come over the horse's back than with a headcollar and two lines.

Minus points:
- The lines are harder to remove and tend to stay around the hocks, which is where they are most worrying for the horse.
- Any tension on the line results in a backward pull on the mouth/nose and there is no possibility of an open rein.
- The lines are set rather low – not in the position the hand would be in, and so can encourage too low a head carriage in some horses (although this lower position is often of great benefit to the horse's back muscles).

Through stirrups, run up and secured
Another good option if you're going on to ride afterwards.

Plus points:
- Lines are higher than if stirrups are down – closer to where hands would be.

Negative points:
- Stirrups are fixed, so don't allow much play of the line through them. This can result in a rather fixed length of rein, rather like side reins.
- Lines may have a tendency to come over horse's back, or even tuck up under the tail (generally unpopular with most horses, who clamp their tails down over the offending line, which never normally helps!)

Roller
These come in a variety of designs, some much more useful than others.

Plus points:
- Great for horses with any sort of muscle wastage. With the addition of a breast girth, the roller doesn't have to be done up very tightly, so there can be absolutely minimal pressure and weight on the horse's back.
- If there are lots of rings, the lines can be attached at whatever height you prefer.
- If the roller has turrets, you can have the lines in the position your hands would be.

Minus points:
- If turrets or higher rings are used, the lines won't pass around the horse's quarters, meaning that the equivalent of the leg aids has effectively been removed. This makes lateral work much more difficult.
- As with stirrups, passing the lines through the rings means that there is no possibility of an open rein.

How to introduce long lines

The primary consideration is safety for both you and the horse. Obvious potential dangers are that you could get kicked, suffer rope burns or get dragged on the lines. The horse could get loose on the lines and panic. I once heard of a horse that collided with a bus while on long lines. I assumed he'd got loose while being long lined on the roads but it turned out he'd panicked in the school, managed to pull away from the trainer and run through the fence and out on to the road. The whole point of long lining is that it is an enjoyable, beneficial, constructive way for you and your horse to work together. If either of you is frightened or injured during the process, it cannot be considered a success!

First of all

Assess your horse. If he's a flighty, unhandled two-year-old and you're thinking a spot of long lining would be a useful part of starting him, please think again. Before you consider long lining a horse like this, it's essential to gain experience with an older, or at least calmer, horse – preferably several older, calmer horses! A horse who wears rugs with leg straps is likely to respond more calmly than a horse who hasn't and would swear he's being attacked by a snake if he sees so much a lead rope lying on the floor. If you think there's any likelihood of your horse being worried by the lines, proceed with great caution and enlist the help of someone who is experienced with long lining a variety of horses.

Use a small, enclosed area to start

It's been said before, but round pens do make life easier. That's why Monty and I take one around with us when we tour, rather than just putting a barrier between the horse and the audience and getting on with it in a wider open space. With 30 feet lines and a pen that's 54 feet in diameter, the chances of the horse getting loose on the lines and panicking are greatly reduced. It's extra work to set up and dismantle the pen for every demonstration, but it's worth it. It would be similarly worth it for you if you were able to use a small enclosure when you first introduce your horse to lines, or transport your horse to a smaller school.

Even in the enclosed area of the pen, the odd horse can be really unsettled by the lines around the quarters. I've come across one or two that cantered around for some time before they were relaxed enough to trot and then walk. With these types you have to keep changing directions constantly so they can't get any speed up and they'll eventually settle down. These were mostly horses with other problems but I was glad I wasn't in a bigger area. My advice is to set everything up so that you're most likely to succeed. Once you've sorted out your small, enclosed area, check it for hazards. Remove any jump wings and obstacles, and anything else that your lines could possibly get caught on. Think 'What could possibly go wrong?' Murphy's Law states that if something can go wrong, it surely will, so do all you possibly can to prevent it – oh, and while you're still learning make sure there are no other horses in the school at the same time!

Body language

I'll be describing the correct body positioning for long lining below, but probably the best way to check out the communication between you and your horse is to do some loose work in the school, and/or a Join Up. If you keep getting unexpected changes of direction, you can be pretty sure you're overtaking the horse, or at least getting too level with his head, or shoulder. At least when the horse is loose, you don't have to deal with the lines and risk getting them in a tangle. Make sure you feel confident that you can direct the horse more or less where you want him to go whilst loose in the school, before you think about attaching lines.

Getting your horse used to the lines

There are two main issues horses tend to have with the lines. One is the feeling of them around their quarters, perhaps reminiscent of dogs snapping at their hocks, and the other is seeing, hearing and feeling the line dragging on the floor behind them, perhaps reminiscent of snakes. You could avoid the former by not putting the lines around the quarters, and instead draping them over the horse's back, but could you guarantee that they would NEVER drop down? Plus you miss out on a lot of the versatility of the lines that way. You could coil the lines up in your hands and so avoid the problem of them dragging on the floor, but this allows for much less sensitivity with the lines, and again, could you promise you would never drop them? It's better to make sure that the horse would be all right with either eventuality.

A good place to start is by checking out how the horse feels about the lines in general. Attach a long line to the Dually, and start to gently

Above: See how disconcerting it feels when you don't really know what people want of you.

lay some coils over the horse's back. Standing close to the horse's shoulder, drape the lines over the horse's quarters. If he seems unconcerned, gently flip the long end of a line over his back, letting it hang down on the other side. Repeat this several times, going over his back and his quarters.

If he's fine with the lines, this will only take a minute or so. If he's not fine, now is a good time to find out. If he does panic or worry at all, go back to something he finds easy, just the lines coiled up for example, and proceed gently until he's confident with the more challenging situation.

There are a variety of ways to introduce the horse to the lines around his quarters. You could try the 'Following Pressure' exercise from *Perfect Manners*. If the horse leaps forwards, he will take the pressure away from his hocks, and as he turns away, you will suddenly find you have just a direct line to his head again. Or you could attach the long line to the Dually on the same side that you're standing, put a few loops on his quarters, and, standing by his shoulder again, drop the coils down over his quarters. If he leaps forwards, again you should be safe and able to bring him back to you. Make sure you have a breast girth as otherwise if the horse kicked out he could pull the roller backwards.

How to long line

Now we're getting to the fun part! Once your horse understands what's happening, long lining is fun and doesn't take at all long to set up. On our courses we start students off long lining each other; sometimes we'll blindfold the 'horse' as well! This is guaranteed to make people a great deal more sensitive to how it is for the horse. Personally I find it

Using body positioning

A few years ago we had a little New Forest pony called Aries to start. He was a very handsome fellow but his owner had been told he was very dangerous and couldn't be broken in. This was on the basis that he was impossible to lunge.

Using the conventional method, with the handler level with the horse and pointing a whip at his quarters, he got confused and moved away out of the circle. When he got pulled back in, he turned and faced the lunger. When this happened, they waved the stick towards his face, which caused him to rear.

He had managed to pull away several times, which prompted them to start lungeing him off the bit. He didn't understand about yielding to the bit, so this wouldn't have helped at all. As it was, he had the most massive pair of wolf teeth I'd ever seen, and the bit pressing against them drove him mad. Using body positioning that made sense to him, he was a pleasure to train – responsive and sensitive, and not at all dangerous.

Recommended Associate Nicole Golding

quite stressful being the 'horse'. You are having to constantly guess what it is that people want. Try it some time for yourself!

When we start youngsters, we use the fact that they intuitively understand body positioning, and this helps them to go on to understand what the pressure from the reins means. We change direction as we would if they were loose and doing a Join Up, and at the same time put a little pressure on the Dually (and then later on the bit) so that they begin to pair the two events in their mind. If we went for just pulling on the Dually, or worse, the horse's mouth at the start, it would put unnecessary pressure on them. Pairing with body language gives them a gentler option when learning.

A fully ridden horse may be a lot less sensitive to your body positioning, and much less worried about any mistakes. He already knows the meaning of the rein aids, in whichever way you normally apply them, so this makes the process a great deal easier. Even so, it's a good idea not to get in your horse's way or to confuse him at all, so here are the recommended aids and positions for long lining:

In the school or pen
If you position yourself behind the horse as you would when out and about on the roads, you will have to run whenever you want your horse to trot or canter. Instead, stay at an angle of 45 degrees to the horse's shoulder. In a school, this means slowing down and dropping back a bit at the corners, because your horse has further to go, and then moving up alongside him for the long sides of the manège.

Circles

These are probably one of the easiest movements on the long line, particularly if your definition of circular is fairly flexible! Come back to circles if your horse is going too fast for you, or you're getting tired, because you move a lot less than the horse does – still a lot more than with conventional lungeing, however. Rather than continuing along the long side, shorten the inside line and move on to a circular track yourself. Practise changing the size of circle. To make it smaller, shorten the inside line. To make it larger, walk towards your horse's girth, making sure you have eye contact.

Think on your feet!

Be aware of the position of your feet – they should be parallel to the sides when moving down the manège. For a circle, your feet should be on the circle, too.

Straight lines

They are much harder than they sound! Make sure that both you and the horse are walking purposefully, keep looking at where you want to go and point your feet in that direction. Correct any deviations from the line quickly before they become too pronounced, but don't apply your aids too strongly or the horse will overcompensate. Try placing some poles on either side of the straight line that you're aiming for as guidelines.

Changes of direction

You can turn the horse across the school in straight lines, on the diagonal, with two half circles or in leg yield, or into the fence, which is a turn about the forehand. Turning across the school simply requires you not to block the horse's inward movement, and to indicate to the horse that you wish him to change direction rather than stay on the circle.

Cheat!

If your horse doesn't understand your body language, cheat and use the lines to make it clear! Don't worry about the bend or finesse at this point. If he thought you meant to ask him to drift into the middle and you wanted him to go down the long side, apply a little pressure to the outside line. The resulting wiggle may look a little drunken but he'll get the idea. If you find you're having difficulty directing him, ask for some assistance. Just make sure your handlers position themselves in such a way that they won't get garrotted, i.e. on the outside of the circle but far enough away from the edge so they won't get squashed either.

Halt

There are two ways to initiate the halt. One is to point him at a wall or fence which brings about a natural halt. With a horse that understands the reins, though, the first aid is to stop walking yourself. If the horse is really paying attention to you, he will stop too, without feeling any pressure on his mouth or nose, just as when he is being led. If he keeps going, however, he will meet resistance from the rein. If he understands how to release himself from pressure, he should stop. It's best not to get into a leaning/pulling match if he doesn't. Keep the contact elastic, so the horse can't get into a dead pull, and release as soon as he stops. You may find it helpful to move your hands in a backwards circle, because when you do that it's very hard for you to pull or the horse to lean. Enlist some help if necessary, or steer the horse into the fence to ask for the halt.

Turn on the forehand

As you approach a corner, overtake the horse and keep eye contact. He will turn away from you into the space in the corner and hence change direction. Once he's got the hang of this in the corner, try it along a straight line. The fence will help him understand that he's not to move forward.

Lateral work

This is easier on the long line than you may think. Make sure the horse understands about moving away from pressure and as a starting point don't aim for perfection, just a movement that is recognizably sideways. As soon as the horse takes a sideways step, praise him and straighten out again. Slowly increase the number of steps until the horse is comfortable with the movement.

There's no such thing as failure...just actions with unintended consequences

If you don't get the reaction you were expecting, ask yourself what you might have done to cause the response you got. Most of the time, horses do what they think we've asked them to do, which might not be what we think we've asked them. Just make a mental note in case it's useful for the future. You wanted a straight line and got a half pass? Well, no point being upset because you can't walk straight – why not see if you can work out how you managed to get that lateral work instead? The horse won't know it isn't what you wanted – and neither will the spectators unless you told them what you were about to do!

However, although it's great to nurture this spirit of discovery and not get upset that you didn't get the result you intended, it is still important to have a sense of purpose. Decide what movement you would like to get and where you would like it to happen; otherwise the exercise can become too meandering, and the horse will sense that you don't know where you want to direct him. This isn't usually inspiring for either of you!

Rein back

Once the horse has come to a complete halt, apply an elastic backwards movement with the reins. It is so important to ask for just one step at a time in the early stages and as soon as the horse even leans in the right direction, release the pressure. If he has any difficulty understanding, use a fence to discourage forward movement, or someone standing in front of him to assist. Build up until the movement is fluid. Remember at all times, your aim is not to force the horse, your aim is to help the horse understand.

Jumping

Don't worry, you don't have to go over the fences yourself! Make sure the lines can't get caught on anything by using blocks and barrels as

Below: Use small steps to give yourself the best chance of success. Here we're taking it literally!

jump wings rather than tall stands. You can put up guiding poles to assist keeping the horse into the jump. Long line off a Dually, so that you can't accidentally pull the horse in the mouth. Start small, say, with trotting poles and gradually work your way up, being careful never to overface your horse.

Roads and tracks

Don't even think about going out on the roads unless you're very confident you can control your horse on long lines. Check this out by long lining around a scary obstacle course in an enclosed area first. Recruit friends who can flap umbrellas at him unexpectedly, and see if you can cope with his response.

When you do decide to venture out, make it as safe as you can. Wear appropriate clothing, including hat, gloves, sturdy footwear, and fluorescent tabards, even if it's a bright day. In the summer in particular,

Accuracy

To start with, don't be too concerned with accuracy. Rather than risking shutting down the horse's energy and enthusiasm, work to gently mould it in the right direction. As you progress you can aspire more to accuracy just as all the top riders do, whether they're eventers going over ever more complicated fences, showjumpers taking the tightest corner, or dressage riders perfecting pirouettes. First things first, though.

Most common problems

Overtaking the horse when circling
This usually happens either because you're used to being in a more central position if you've traditionally lunged, or because your enthusiasm gets the better of you and you find yourself moving faster in the middle than the horse is on the outside. Chances are if this is happening to you, your horse will be stopping or making unexpected changes of direction. Another example of the horse telling you all you need to know about your mistakes!

Getting in a muddle with the lines
When the horse changes direction, the line that was around his quarters now goes straight to you (or through the stirrup and straight to you) and so you need to take up the slack. The line that was going directly to the horse needs to be let out to go around the horse's quarters. This sort of adjustment is very hard to make if the lines are coiled up, so generally I leave the ends on the floor when the horse is circling in the round pen. Keep the ends of the lines on the inside of you so they don't start to wrap around your legs. When you need to take up slack, hold both lines in one hand and use your spare hand to gather the loose line. To let the line out, simply let it slip through your hand.

Finding it hard to direct the horse
If your horse doesn't seem to have a clue what you want and wanders about all over the school, you are both in danger of ending up tangled like spaghetti in the lines. Try getting a friend to help you by leading you in some circles, straight lines and figures of eight. This may make the patterns clearer to the horse, so they seem much less random to him. On the other hand, you may find it works to make it a bit more demanding. You could try putting out trotting poles to long line over and cones to bend through. Having something specific to concentrate on can help at times.

**Above: A student long
lining Pie with me –
'It is better to ask some
questions than to know all
the answers.'**

James Thurber

it can be hard to see a horse against a tree in full leaf, and the sooner
the traffic sees you, the easier it is for drivers to slow down in time.
Ideally, choose quiet roads at quiet times, and bring a friend who can
assess the traffic situation for you (i.e. go ahead around blind corners),
and clip a lead rope onto the horse whenever it is needed. I know this
isn't very labour efficient, and the idea is that the horse becomes bold
because he has to walk out in front of you, but unless he is absolutely
perfect, you'll appreciate the support on the ground, particularly in the
early days.

Only consider venturing out on to the roads alone if you know that
you can easily go from the driving to leading position without the lines
getting tangled up, and that the horse is fine in all traffic. Make sure
too that the horse is unconcerned about the lines dragging behind
him, so that if he should become loose (say if you tripped over, fell
and dropped the lines), he won't panic and feel like he's being pur-
sued by them.

Emergency stop

If the horse does take off very fast due to a fright, don't attempt to hold him back on both lines. You'll soon realise you will not be able to hold him and you're likely to go skiing along the road with him. In this real emergency scenario, where your only other option is to let go of the lines (not good), the best strategy is to drop one line and hold on strongly to the other. This effectively 'jack knifes' the horse or, more technically, 'disengages his hind quarters', bringing him round to face you. It's preferable not to have to do this but it's an effective method for emergencies. The best rein to hold on to is usually the left one, because it will bring the horse into the edge of the road rather than into the middle. Keep calm and undo any lines that are getting in the way. Be aware that if you're long lining from a bit, this may put considerable pressure on the horse's mouth, but that's a lot better than having him loose on the road. This is why I encourage you to introduce him to as many things as you can think of that might spook him in the safety of the school before venturing out.

Muddly lines and tiny corrections

When people are not used to working with lines they tend to get them in a muddle. Experienced people generally don't get them in such a muddle. I asked myself why would that be? I commissioned a study on this (well I casually asked IH Recommended Associate Julia Fisher what she thought and we both agreed). It's the same as the difference between tidy people and untidy people, there is no difference; except that tidy people keep tidying up as they go along. This same theory applies with riding (maybe everything!), you look and think 'She's a great rider, it's so easy for her!' but the point you mustn't miss is that she is likely to be making tiny corrections all the time, and that's why she's as good as she is. When you are less experienced you just have to keep reminding yourself to keep making the corrections necessary until they become automatic.

Key points

- Long lining is an educational and physically useful exercise in many situations and with many different types of horses and ponies.
- Long lining equipment can vary greatly; choose only the equipment that is relevant to you and your horse.
- Make sure you introduce your horse to lines sensitively and safely.
- Use your body language and rein aids to control your horse's speed and direction.
- Make sure you fully understand where you need to be positioned – perhaps practise with a human first!
- Practise in a safe, enclosed area before getting more adventurous.
- Be sure you know how the 'emergency stop' works, should it be needed.
- Once you're confident, introduce your horse to spooky obstacles, ground poles, jumping and many interesting new challenges.

Teaching your horse to be brave (without scaring yourself in the process)

There are people who say things like, '"Failure" never enters my vocabulary', or 'There is no such thing as failure only "learning experiences".' While I applaud such positive attitudes, personally I feel there are some 'learning experiences' one can do without – those occasions when bodily parts get bruised, battered or broken are generally best avoided. Worse still is getting your horse hurt (horses are harder to fix, there's no National Health treatment for them and, worst of all, you go through a huge amount of guilt), and it was with this in mind that I added the chapter subtitle 'without scaring yourself in the process'.

Nobody is denying that if you are a really strong, experienced rider you may be able to use brute force and fear to get your horse to do what you want. It's worth noting, though, that many strong and experienced riders are choosing a more thoughtful approach of their own accord. This 'Intelligent Approach' could also be called the 'over-30s approach', or whatever that birthday is when a sudden sense of self-preservation starts to appear. Whether you're 11, 17 or 23 years old, this approach is equally appropriate if you'd like to take a more thoughtful and sensitive line with your horse.

Our aim is to have a horse that is brave and reliable. A horse that is forced to perform through fear and punishment will only continue while he can see no other option. As soon as he has a 'weaker' rider on him or his usual rider has an off-day, he'll take charge of the situation immediately. If you've been unfortunate enough to buy, for instance, a showjumper who was successful for his previous rider due to harsh treatment but won't jump at all for you, it's no

This approach doesn't mean you can't be brave, brilliant and anything on earth you want to be. It just means you don't have to break your neck to prove it.

good blaming it on the horse's ingratitude. It's a very natural occurrence. Some people send the horse away to be 'beaten up' and he'll perform again for perhaps one or two shows before he then resumes what's called 'dirty stopping': this is where it feels to the rider as if the horse is going to jump but he then stops at the very last minute, often pitching the rider into the fence. If you have a horse like this my advice is that he should be completely reschooled from scratch. He should jump because he's happy to jump, not because he's frightened of being whipped or spurred. That way you'll both have a much safer and more pleasurable time.

Where to start – at the beginning perhaps? When teaching your horse to be brave it's a good idea to work out what point you are starting from, and where it is you aim to get to. For my part, these were my key aims with my horse Pie in January 2003:

1 I wanted him not to feel that he had to shy violently at any stones he thought shouldn't be there.

2 I wanted him to be sensible enough for my niece Daisy to ride him at some shows.

3 I wanted him to jump reliably, i.e. without running out or stopping randomly.

Once aims 1, 2 and 3 were coming into place, another goal formed:

4 I wanted him to be bold enough to jump the Working Hunter courses that Daisy now wanted to ride him in, including jumping water, ditches, hedges and walls.

Exercise – write down

What stage would you say you are at now? Where would you like to get to: as a first stage (i.e. just the simplest improvements)? As a second stage (i.e. a little more ambitious)? Would there be a third stage if you achieved stages one and two?

All the steps outlined in this chapter are designed to suit an average rider who has to fit in time with her horse after working hours (sometimes when it's getting dark, especially in the winter!). However, in order for the two of you to gain confidence in each other it helps if you could spend as much time as possible together. By this I mean that riding or handling for at least one hour a day will give you much better results than just 'fitting your horse in' on the occasional weekend. I guess that's a fact with most relationships. We all have the same 24 hours in a day – we each must decide how we want to prioritise that time to create a Perfect Partnership.

Let's look first at a common problem.

Everyday spooking and shying

I mentioned before how easy it is to assume the horse is doing something – like spooking/shying/making a fuss – 'for no reason at all'. But how can such a conclusion ever improve the situation? It's a truly unhelpful point of view. You are much better off thoroughly exploring any possible causes as, a) you could get it right and, b) it keeps you positively focused, and less likely to get frustrated and act foolishly, possibly even doing something you'd regret and that would only make the situation worse. Let's say you could absolutely prove the horse was doing something undesirable 'for no reason at all' – if you said to the horse, 'I know for certain you are doing this for no reason at all', would he say to you, 'I am sorry. You are correct. I have been doing this just to be silly. I apologise and won't do it again.' It's unlikely.

Spooking and shying in horses, although it can be due to too much energy, is not 'naughtiness' or something they think up on a whim. It's actually an inherent part of their nature. Their quick reactions have helped them to survive the six million or so years they have been around. Furthermore, it's possible that by spooking and shying, a well-meaning horse may think he's protecting you. He doesn't understand that he's putting you more at risk. Certainly, if you were on safari in Africa, would you rather be on the alert horse that looks out for lions in the bush, or the one that stands steady while the black rhino's charging at you? This doesn't make the horse that spooks at a plastic bag any less dangerous or uncomfortable, but it's important to look at things from the horse's point of view. If you have a sympathetic attitude, you can work towards building your horse's confidence and ability to focus. Perhaps, too, he'll then be able to distinguish between those situations that are dangerous, and those that aren't.

> A spooky, hyper-alert horse can give you one of the most valuable educations you can ever have around horses. He can help you pick out the details of how a horse sees the world. You can start to learn what that's like – what a wonderful gift to have!

Eyesight

It's important to appreciate how horses' eyesight differs from ours, not just in placement and peripheral vision but also in the fact that they can pick out the tiniest movement, often initially imperceptible to the human eye. You may be familiar with this scenario. You're riding along on a very quiet day, thinking nothing could possibly distract your horse, when suddenly he stops dramatically, head bolt upright. You can feel his heart pounding. You look to where he's looking and can't see anything unusual at all. Then if you look really, really carefully, you can see someone going along on a bicycle, probably about four miles away.

Horses seem able to study outlines more than fine detail. This could explain why even when they know perfectly well who you are they suddenly go into shock when they see you with a rucksack on your back or pushing a wheelbarrow.

I remember going to visit Pie in his early days before he came to live with me. He was turned out and walking along the field quite happily when he suddenly saw an upside-down wheelbarrow and jumped up on all four feet in total amazement. He'd seen the wheelbarrow every day for months and had never even acknowledged it when it had been the right way up. Whatever was he thinking when it was tipped over? He'd just come over from Ireland – maybe leprechauns live under turned over wheelbarrows out there?

Exercise – do *try this at home*
Hold up your index finger about six to eight inches from your nose. Alternately, open and close left and right eyes while focusing on your finger. Your finger appears to move a couple of inches against the background. When your horse sees an object out of one eye and then turns quickly to see it with the other eye, the object appears to move, thus causing the 'shy' reflex in the untrained horse. He'll then often turn to try to get a look at the thing with both eyes, using his binocular vision, which helps him judge the distance of the object.

For this reason, round-pen or Join Up work can be very useful with horses that spook and shy. It educates them from both sides, as well as introducing them to changing sights and sounds from around the front and back ends, in a safe, secure environment.

Let the horse see the danger moving away
Saffron, a pony I worked with for the BBC1 programme *Barking Mad*, was frightened of bicycles. I did several gentle Join Ups with him so he understood that I would invite him in and he could be safe and comfortable following me. Then one day I took Saffron into the round pen and very gently followed him with a bike. He moved away immediately with his tail in the air, snorting as he trotted around. After a while, he slowed

down and started looking at me and I immediately dropped my eyes and wheeled the bike away from him. This advance and retreat technique gives the pony a feeling of control. The theory is that horses know an object, or person, can't be dangerous if it moves away because no predator would ever move away from a prey animal – once a predator moves in, it kills. The method certainly works well for introducing a horse to a suitable scary object, in this case a bike. It was fascinating to see Saffron encounter some bikes when he was next out in the open, he immediately started following them!

If your horse is frightened of traffic behind him, it's a good idea to turn him round to face it going past and then turn back so he can see it moving away from him. It will help him feel more secure. In fact, you can use this strategy to help your horse overcome his fear of most naturally moving subjects, including people, cows and other animals, as well as traffic.

Desensitization

This means gradually getting the horse used to the object that scares him so that, in the end, he accepts it totally. You could turn your horse out in a round pen, or similar safe, enclosed area, with some plastic bags, sheep or whatever it is he's frightened of a little distance away, and allow him to eat and relax there. Sometimes it's useful to touch the horse gently with the scary object. I prefer to have my horse on a Dually halter with this training. I have more control than with just a regular headcollar and I don't risk hurting his mouth as I would if I used a bridle and bit. If he's frightened of plastic bags a good way to desensitize him to these is stroking him with a small plastic or paper bag firmly tied to the end of a stick. You do your best to remove it before he objects or gets frightened. To start with you may not even touch him but just see how close you can get it before his adrenalin levels rise. The idea is that he feels that *he* is training the bag, i.e. if he stands still the bag goes away. You can gradually use bigger bags and move quite fast and he'll be completely unconcerned.

The importance of checking your horse's eyesight

I've had personal experience of this recently. The mare that I ride is a spooky sort of girl anyway – 'alert' I like to call her! – but this winter she got dramatically worse. Luckily her owner is caring enough to know that Violet wasn't just playing up and called the vet for a check-up. It turned out that she had had an eye infection (with no outward symptoms) which had damaged both of her eyes so that it was like she was seeing through a milky veil. No wonder normally worrying things suddenly became terrifying for her. For a while we thought she might need surgery but, thankfully, the worst of the damage was cleared up with eyedrops, and though her eyesight may never be 100 per cent again, it has improved enough that she is more or less back to her 'normal' spooky self!

Bonita Hall, Holder of the Monty Roberts
Preliminary Certificate of Horsemanship

Right: Monty Roberts and Ian Vandenberghe desensitizing a police horse using a plastic bag on a stick.

It is very important to take things really slowly so that there is no chance of taking the horse beyond a level with which he can cope. The whole point of these exercises is to increase the horse's confidence in what he is capable of and perhaps, if necessary, increase the handler's confidence at the same time.

The difference between sensitizing and desensitizing horses

If a horse is sensitive and a bit jumpy, the tendency is to move around him very carefully and to barely move your legs or reins when riding him in case you make him jump. If a horse is lazy we tend to kick and push him on with much more vigour. This seems a perfectly sensible course to take and in the early stages it makes sense. However, if it carries on, the oversensitive horse is going to become more sensitive and the unresponsive horse is likely to become more unresponsive.

This is an example of counter-intuitive actions being appropriate – think how you would naturally behave and then do the opposite! The over-sensitive horse would benefit from you moving around him more freely and making sure he is completely comfortable with your everyday movements and scary objects that appear around the place. The lazy horse needs to know that he must react more quickly to requests. If you ask him, for instance, to move over and he just ignores you, step up the pressure immediately, so that he really takes you more seriously the first time.

Does your horse fall into either of these categories? Are you training him to be better or worse?

Help your horse to feel secure

The more secure a horse feels with you, the more relaxed he will be. You have to find a way to manage your horse so that he doesn't feel the need to be constantly on guard.

It's important to build a strong bond with your horse. When a jumpy horse is sent to me, I usually do several Join Ups over the course of a few days, followed by some more training from the ground in the round pen. Then I go through some halter work, building up to the point where I can take him over tarpaulin and around 'scary objects' with no bother at all.

> 'I'm grateful for all my problems. As each of them was overcome I became stronger and more able to meet those yet to come. I grew on my difficulties.'
>
> **J.C. Penney, American retailing magnate**

Following this sort of routine will help to develop the trust between the pair of you. Use lots of praise and relaxation breaks so the sessions are enjoyable for him. Remember to breathe deeply and evenly yourself. Tell him what a champion he is. Each success will give him more confidence. The discipline of waiting for your instructions in the halter work as to where to place his feet are really going to help his mindset. Soon you will be able to transfer this discipline to his ridden work.

When soldiers are caught by the enemy it must be quite terrifying. How do they cope? They have it drilled into them that they are to give their name, rank and serial number only. They are taught to run a mantra through their head under questioning. It could be a prayer, a poem, anything. They have to repeat it in their minds over and over again to avoid allowing in the negative words of the enemy.

What has this got to do with spooky horses? The principle's the same. You need to train your horse in a safe environment to focus totally on you for when the time comes that it becomes seriously important. Work on your lateral moves, half halts, rein backs, relaxing the head in either direction. You have your horse for pleasure rides? Is it really necessary to spend precious hacking time drilling him to focus his total attention on you? Well, just imagine for a minute that you are riding down your normal quiet country road when you see a juggernaut hurtling towards you far too fast. Would you prefer to leave it to fate or to go into 'discipline mode'? 'I'm going to ask him for a lateral move to the left now, a half halt, position his head slightly to the right and, keeping my right leg on strongly, I'm riding forward'. Being able to get the horse 100 per cent focused on you at a time like that can pre-empt a shy and could save your lives. It's necessary to think and practise before an emergency occurs. I recently heard of a boy who was grabbed by a crocodile in Darwin, Australia, which was an unusual thing to happen in that part of the country. The boy was saved because he remembered his teacher's advice at school – he jabbed the crocodile in the eyes and it let him go. Now, if that's not a good advertisement for thinking these things out ahead I don't know what is!

Learn to anticipate these little challenges that are going to come up, particularly with a youngster, and if you see something your horse is likely to spook at, focus your attention way past that object and ride on. I learned from a great trainer, Charlie Edwards in Shropshire, that when showjumping against the clock, once you've jumped a fence, immediately look at the next one because your horse will naturally follow your eyes. This was illustrated perfectly one day as I was cantering along some gallops in Lambourn. The gallops were really wide, about 30 metres (that's about 32 yards), and as we were cantering along I saw a sign in the distance. I was looking at it, wondering what it said – as we got closer I could see it said clearly 'No Cantering' – and can you believe what happened? In spite of all that space we nearly ran straight into the sign! I remembered then – the horse will take you where you're looking.

'When your horse shies at an object and is unwilling to go up to it, he should be shown that there is nothing fearful in it, least of all to a courageous horse like him, but if this fails, touch the object yourself that seemed so dreadful to him, and lead him up to it with gentleness.' *Xenophon, who was no sentimentalist with horses, wrote this 23 centuries ago.*

Once you've gained your horse's trust on the ground it can be transferred to you as a rider as well. In the herd if something frightens the group, they all look up and stare immediately. Once the leader has taken a look, decided there is nothing to worry about and resumed grazing, the rest go back to grazing. If you're not worried, why should your horse be? The best way to reassure your horse is to act unconcerned. Singing is an excellent idea because it ensures you are breathing correctly. If actually you are a little concerned but still feel it's the right thing for you to be riding him in this particular situation you use the great 'as if' technique, which I first learned about when I had to do my first public speaking (terrifying!). You simply act as if you are a very confident, relaxed person – sounds crazy, but I can vouch that it really can work!

If your horse spooks, shies or stops unexpectedly on a ride, be sure you don't punish him because that will give him all the more reason to be frightened and mistrust you further. Also, do try to stay on because having the rider fall off is quite unnerving for a sensitive horse! You have to decide what is the most appropriate action to take with your particular horse in the particular situation you are in. It may be best to wait quietly with him, or it may be best to start making some turns in the opposite direction in a nonchalant manner. Some rein back may be the right course to take.

Left: 'You will do foolish things, but do them with enthusiasm!'

Colette

TEACHING YOUR HORSE TO BE BRAVE

Why it's good to think ahead – the story of Cookie

November is summertime in Australia and it was hot; in fact, it was very hot. The country was experiencing a serious drought to the extent that herds of kangaroo were coming into the suburban areas looking for water and a bit of green grass on some of the irrigated acreage. When there is a drought in Australia, there is inevitably high fire danger. Making it even worse, eastern Australia is virtually covered with eucalyptus trees, which burn like torches.

Horse owners tend to live on properties outside of the cities, and thus are surrounded by eucalyptus forests. When a fire sweeps through rural properties, the loss of homes, animals and even people is often devastating. My tour organizer, Tara King, and her husband Scott had recently experienced a very close call. To ensure the safety of their animals, Tara had transported them to safer facilities several miles away while Scott stood guard over the house. Fortunately, though, the fire swept around their property and it was spared.

While I was in the Sydney area, Tara came to me saying that a friend of hers had called to ask her a favour. She had a friend, Sally Tucker, who lived on a property near Galston, a heavily forested area that was in great danger during this hot, dry season. Sally owned several horses, including a gelding named Cookie. She had no problem with her other horses should she have to evacuate the property because of approaching fire, but as for Cookie, she knew he would have to stay behind and face the consequences.

The reason Cookie couldn't be evacuated is that he simply would not load in a trailer. As I was in the area I put aside a morning to devote to Cookie and his phobia.

Cookie was a very nice horse in almost every way, except where horse trailers were concerned. When it came to trailers, Cookie was a monster. I suppose it took me nearly ten minutes to load Cookie after I had done my normal ten to fifteen minutes of communication prior to taking him to the vehicle. In my demonstrations, the average time to load after communication is less than a minute. Cookie was nearly ten times tougher than most of my horses at public events.

I spent nearly an hour with Sally and Cookie, instructing both regarding the elements of loading, and left feeling I'd put my best effort in to ensuring her chances of success in the future. I was still concerned, though, because you never know how it will go until there is a need to perform at a time of crisis. Should an evacuation become necessary, how much more nervous would Sally be? Would the noise from the burning trees make it much more frightening for Cookie?

Just a couple of weeks later, while I was on tour in New Zealand, word came through to us that a wild fire had roared through Galston. All the animals and people were forced to evacuate their properties. It was so good to hear that when Sally led Cookie to the trailer, he loaded without hesitation and was transported without a hitch to safe surroundings with friends nearby.

It isn't often that circumstances prove without doubt how necessary it is to take some time to develop trust and co-operation with your horse. In this case, however, it was a matter of life or death. It's good to think that the short time taken on that baking November morning resulted in 'life'.

Monty Roberts

I used to ride a racehorse who would spin round violently. His name, appropriately, was Lightning. I'd stop his spin as quickly as I could, then ask him to rein back a few steps, relax and walk on quietly. After I had used this exercise for a while, if he saw something he felt was suspicious he would still dramatically tense up to whip round the other way, but suddenly he'd remember the drill. After hesitating for a second, he would take a couple of respectful steps backwards and then continue as if nothing had happened. After a while he got out of his dangerous habit completely.

If you're leading your horse when a scary object is encountered, turn a few circles, touch the item yourself and give your horse a nice reassuring rub. If you're riding, just act as if you're not bothered at all. After taking a look at the item, studiously ignore it and slowly circle your horse in front of or around it until you feel his pulse rate is right down. You don't need to force him too close. – that might seem like a punishment at this stage – you're just working to build up his confidence. Ride on a light contact at most.

It's a great advantage to get a young horse confident with different things early in life.

If he feels as though he's going to break into a trot, just turn him in small circles, crossing one rein over his wither in a relaxed fashion until he settles down. Have a neck strap if you feel you may be tempted to grab something for security, much better to hold a neck strap than tightly on your horse's mouth. If you feel worried that you're not holding him tight enough and he may put his head down, hold the reins short but put your hands forward. That way his head is free and you'll feel safer, if it's not horse psychology we use, it's rider psychology!

I am not suggesting that you can 'cure' every horse of his fears within a matter of weeks to ensure he will never shy again. Some horses are always more likely than others to take you, and themselves, by surprise – but it does keeps you awake and is *so* good for your seat! As a person with a fairly high 'startle response' myself (my brother still thinks it's hilarious to pounce from behind doors shouting 'boo!' to make me jump in the air), I know it will always be part of my make-up, but if I have a reasonable knowledge of what's happening around me and I feel secure in a place, I'm unlikely to be startled. With your horse the more you follow the exercises to build up his confidence, the rarer his spooky occurrences will be. Remember the 'magic is in the mix' and keep your learning curve together fun. Keep building your horse's self-esteem and confidence while also working to ensure he focuses on you, particularly in times of concern. Soon your horse will be proud to show you how brave he is!

Introducing your horse to specific tricky obstacles, both natural and totally unnatural

1 Start with a well-schooled horse
Your horse should be responsive to your aids in general. If he doesn't move off your leg or stop as asked before you introduce him to the

scary object, he's not suddenly going to become soft and obedient as his adrenalin levels start to rise. In fact, quite the opposite will happen. Even if he is well schooled, he could become quite wooden as he is introduced to the new objects.

Lateral aids are important, too. Ideally, you want to be able to position your horse's front or back end wherever you like, so as well as leg yielding, turns on the forehand and turns on the haunches are useful exercises.

If you start from the ground, which I recommend, use the right equipment. A well-fitting Dually halter is ideal for this sort of work and, just as important, a long enough rope or long rein. You need a minimum of 12ft to keep control in the event of the horse jumping away sharply. The nearer to his head you are holding him, the more your arm will be jerked and the greater the likelihood of you getting pulled over, trodden on or injured.

Find a safe area to work in. A round pen is commonplace in nearly every American or Australian yard and can be invaluable from the point

Right: 'Curiosity is one of the permanent and certain characteristics of a vigorous intellect.'
Samuel Johnson

Opposite: 'Jump!'
Joseph Campbell

of view of safety as all your problems are contained! If you haven't got a round pen, evaluate the risk. What is the worst that can happen if your horse gets loose? If he'll be in an enclosed yard, or small field, that's fine. If he could tear off and get on to a main road, that's unacceptable.

If things don't go quite to plan, perhaps you are asking too much too soon. Try taking your horse out with a steady, reliable lead horse for a few months to give him confidence. Gradually your horse will grow braver and you can take over the lead in suitable circumstances until you are ready to go out on your own.

2 Don't feel bad jumping off and leading him past, or through, difficult areas

It's tempting to think this may be 'giving in' and 'the horse will know he's won' but, in fact, it gives the horse confidence. This strategy causes far less damage to your relationship with your horse, as well as being safer, than trying to whip him past something he's still frightened of, which may cause him to lose trust in you. Ideally, once you've led a horse past something a couple of times, remount and ride him past until he's completely habituated to the object and wonders what all the fuss was about.

> 'A problem well stated is a problem half solved.'
>
> **Charles Franklin Kettering, American engineer and inventor**

Safety rules for working from the ground

- Wear a hard hat and sturdy footwear. Gloves can prevent rope burns. Remove rings to prevent a rope wrapping around your finger and breaking it, or worse.
- Keep a safe distance. For this, a good length of rope is essential.
- If you're working in an open area, a lunge rein can be better than rope, so that if he really pulls away, he's able to go a little distance without jerking you. Then you can reel him in. However, working with a longer line does have problems – it's hard to keep tangle free and NEVER WRAP A LINE AROUND YOUR HAND OR ARM.
- Keep an eye on the horse at all times. This is not the same as looking him in the eye. It just means you should be aware of where he is at any given time. Until you are completely confident in your horse, you are often better off keeping your body turned slightly towards him when leading him near a scary object.
- Evaluate the situation before you start. Should the horse be startled and jump, *you don't want him to jump on you!* Do be sure that you position yourself accordingly. If you are leading him past a scary obstacle, *expect him to shy away from it.* Stay on the same side as the obstacle so he shies away from you and not on top of you.
- Ensure you're not going to be trapped between your horse and anything solid, e.g. a fence or a wall. Crushing comes under the 'not good' label!
- Even with these precautions some insecure horses do actually aim to jump in your lap, Scooby Doo-style, which is really not advisable. Keep an eye on your horse and be prepared to use assertive body language if necessary, e.g. square up and look him in the eye and shake the rope to keep him away from you.

3 Long line your horse

This is an excellent way to increase your horse's self-confidence and independence – and excellent exercise for you. Work through the exercises on this (Chapter 5), and don't forget to ask a friend who is experienced with horses to go with you on your first few training walks. Your friend can walk by your horse's head and help if you run into any problems.

> You can't command a horse not to be frightened but you can teach him acceptable ways to behave when he is frightened.

If things are still not going right

One reason may be that he's getting too much food and not enough exercise. Although it's no fun riding a tired or lethargic horse (certainly no fun for the horse), high spirits have to be kept within acceptable limits. A horse that is constantly on his toes and looking around all over the place may not be 'just enjoying himself' as is often expressed, but could be in a constant state of anxiety and stress.

An experienced owner should know the difference and feed and exercise her horse appropriately. It's easy to get caught out, though, and many of us have a tendency to show our love through food. There's something very satisfying about mixing up bits and pieces for your horse and some of the muesli mixes look good enough for human consumption. However, for some horses, overfeeding certain foods is akin to giving them rocket fuel. Pie, being hyperactive, has taught me so much about this. Last year he was going so nicely that I thought a double handful of 'quiet mix' in his feed 'wouldn't hurt now'. The very next day he started his dramatic 'rock spooking' again. Having the right feed balance can influence your horse's behaviour massively. Get to know how your horse's droppings usually look so you can note any changes that indicate stress and possibly gastric ulcers or digestive upsets.

> Horses will learn what to be frightened of and what not to be frightened of from each other as well as from you.

Another reason for lack of success is that the horse has no confidence in the rider, which may be the case if the rider is very inexperienced and/or nervous and/or gives contradictory and confusing signals. For the doubtful rider, there's no substitute for hard work and practice in the long term but in the short term what can help is seeing someone else ride the horse over the ditch/past the obstacle. The rider can then feel confident that the task is possible.

> 'We cannot solve the problems we have created with the same thinking that created them.'
>
> **Albert Einstein**

It's extra-helpful for a less confident rider to go past the obstacle on a rock-solid reliable horse. This would let her know that she has the ability to do what is required. There's an old saying that 'good horses make good jockeys'. While the tricky horse can teach you so much when you're ready for those challenges, I've seen many a good old schoolmaster of a horse turn a poor rider into a successful one by boosting her confidence.

Secret of success – it's as simple as making a plan

Now we come to the secret of making your horse totally immune to scary obstacles, smells and sounds. Simply make his training in this area a priority. If you want to make a difference, make a plan.

Success story number one

An impressive result was achieved by one of our Intelligent Horsemanship Recommended Associates, Dan Wilson, in Cornwall. He'd always done a great job of starting young horses but when he decided to get a young pony ready for his three-year-old daughter, Lauren, you could tell there was a quantum leap in leaving nothing to chance! Not only was the pony completely desensitized to traffic, plastic bags and noise, but he was also trained to stand still if his rider fell off. Dan rigged up a dummy to fall off at chosen moments and the pony soon learned to stop as soon as the dummy started to lose balance. The pony was also trained to stand unbothered as the dummy was pulled through his legs.

Watch out for the spring grass coming through

If you find your horse gets more excitable at this time of year, it may be due to the lack of magnesium and the added sugars in the grass. Dairy farmers know all about this because cows can suffer from 'staggers' due to lack of magnesium. Horse owners should be aware of it, too, and be prepared to supplement magnesium as necessary to keep their horses on an even keel.

Success story number two

Monty Roberts was asked to provide six mustangs to take part in the 1 January Rose Bowl Parade through the streets of Los Angeles. He knew this would be the ultimate test for these little horses, with big crowds, noise, waving flags and, worst of all, kids throwing firecrackers. Apparently, some horses could be really upset by the kids' toy 'crazy string', although it was harmless. Monty's people worked for two months to accustom the mustangs to what they might expect and they behaved impeccably, walking along in the parade for two hours.

The Pie Plan

To get Pie sensible enough for Daisy to ride in competitions, he had to feel comfortable with large crowds around. When I first had him at home in the summer of 2001, I rode him over to the Lambourn fair to let him take a look. With eyes on stalks he was managing to hold it together and for obvious reasons I was keeping him well away from all the people but still I managed to achieve one of the most embarrassing moments of my life. A very nice, friendly young man (we used to call him 'Tom Cruise' locally) saw me and strolled over (he obviously didn't read horses very well) and said, 'Oh hello, it's Pie isn't it?' Before I had time to warn him, 'Be a bit careful. He's very excited,' he went to give Pie a stroke and Pie in his excitement headbutted him with such force I fully expected him to drop down on the spot. Happily, Tom Cruise managed to stay on his feet although he did say, 'I must be getting off now,' in a somewhat dazed manner.

> 'Every difficulty slurred over will be a ghost to disturb your repose later on.'
>
> **Frederick Chopin**

With hindsight (a wonderful thing), I should have had someone with me to warn friendly people to keep away. As always, it's important to do a risk assessment – 'What's the worst that can happen?', 'How would I handle that?' Safety is paramount for you, other people and your horse. Once you are completely sure that members of the public are absolutely safe, one of the most important parts of the plan is to keep the main focus of your attention and concern on the horse. Getting embarrassed about how your horse 'should' be behaving, but isn't, is just a hindrance. Don't allow yourself to be distracted by worrying about what other people might think or whether 'he is deliberately making a fool of me' (he's not, he's just being a horse).

Of course, this becomes more an of issue when you are out with your horse in public. Among the many problems people write to me about, 'my horse is ring shy' is not unusual, or 'my horse jumps so nicely at home but as soon as he gets in the ring he just gets faster and faster/rushes'. In that case, it's a question of getting your horse to feel as relaxed in the ring as he is at home. My advice is compete *Hors Concours,* i.e. you ask the judge's permission to go in the show ring for experience rather than as a competitor. This way you can be prepared to stop, circle, back up or whatever is necessary to let your horse know that the rules between the two of you are just the same even if a bell has rung and there are other people around.

With Pie I saw the ideal opportunity in April 2002 of getting him 'crowd-proofed' and persuaded Monty Roberts he should come along on tour with us so the spectators could see a ridden 'work in progress'. So that everyone was absolutely clear that I was not showing a 'finished horse' I wore a bright yellow sweatshirt stating 'Work in Progress' on it. Pie was asked to go through some simple manoeuvres and I was very proud of him, although the audience could clearly see that he was inexperienced and there was plenty of work still to do.

In the interval we let people come and meet him, and he was very relaxed about that. The deal was he could eat hay at the same time if he agreed to acknowledge politely all and sundry who came up to say hello! Chewing is a great relaxant in itself and the horse's stomach is not designed to be empty for any length of time, so it was an ideal way to encourage him to feel comfortable with lots of people around. By the seventh and last demonstration of that tour he was getting quite good and that summer I took him to two BHS Trec competitions (a three-stage competition with an orienteering stage, control of paces and an obstacle section) where he got top marks both times in the obstacle section. Sadly he never really mastered the navigation section...

In July 2003 Daisy rode Pie in their first competition together since Pie had turned over his new leaf. The last time Daisy had ridden Pie a couple of years before, when he was kept at a yard local to her, he had bucked her off six times in one session. That's when Auntie Kelly got the ride – one of the best things that ever happened to me. After a year or so, I thought it would be nice for the two of them to get together again, especially as Daisy didn't have a horse to ride at the time. Also Pie needs plenty of exercise, otherwise he has to be in the starvation paddock all summer and people call him 'Pork Pie', which is very annoying. As far as Pie is concerned, one of the bonuses of travelling is that he always has a full haynet in the horsebox, which makes it one of his favourite places.

After watching me go over the practice jump a few times, Daisy got on and they went in the clear-round jumping (about 1ft maximum height). They went clear and he was fairly settled – he pretty much trot-ted round – and horse and rider gained more confidence in one another. 'Hmm, well, we could take him to Chepstow Show next week.'

Opposite: Monty Roberts and Pie meeting the children of Kingshurst Junior School.

Relax the horse in a crowd

Many years ago I had a nice ex-racehorse to showjump in affiliated classes. Our first few novice classes went well until we got to Hickstead when he just seemed to 'boil over' in the class. At that time they had a clear-round jumping in one of the outer rings. It cost £5 a time to enter, which seemed a fortune then (actually, it was a fortune then!). I took him in, spent ages trotting him between the fences, thanked the judge very much and came out. They probably thought I was mad! I spent another £10 doing much the same again although I ended up jumping a couple of fences. He was really relaxed by this time. The next Foxhunters class I entered I was second to the wonderful Caroline Bradley and she said what a lovely jumper he was.

It was so worthwhile to spend the time not competing and not worrying about what other people might think, just for that moment.

There were just three entries in the Working Hunter Pony with jumps at about 2ft 6in, and being the only clear they won – so horse and rider confidence went up another degree!

Although Daisy and Pie had a few of their own 'learning curves' that summer, the partnership was getting better and better. In fact, their year couldn't have ended much better as Daisy ended up winning the British Show Pony Society Rider of the Year on Pie, but that upgrading brought a whole new set of challenges.

Pie now had to be prepared to jump the far scarier obstacles that are used for the Open Working Hunter classes. This is the pony that was shying at rocks not so long ago. Once he's familiar with something he's fine, but it's almost as though his brain takes a little longer to work out what his eyes are seeing than everyone else's. If he can't take in what he's seeing, he stops *way* out, with heart pounding and ears pricked, trying to figure out what on earth the something is. The common way to deal with this is to administer a few smacks of the whip, but this is not going to stop a horse being frightened. In fact, it's very likely to make things worse. Even if he jumps, he's likely to be unbalanced, which could cause a mishap. Some horses that know they'll be hit for hesitating go full speed into the jump and then stop, ducking out at the last minute. Remember, the aim is to achieve our goals in the safest way, least reliant on strength and bravery, and so my course was to work at familiarizing Pie with as many different options as possible.

Obstacles and challenges

Many of the causes of problems and suggestions on how to overcome them given here can apply to several situations, so do read all the sections to ensure you are getting a complete picture, and think through how best to deal with a particular problem with your horse.

Going through water

If you have gained your horse's trust, he 'should' be prepared to go through water and into unknown territory. However, if he is still nervous, find a way to make it easy for him to do what you want him to do. For instance, lead him through very shallow water to start with, or follow an older, more experienced horse. When he's done that once, you've really got to capitalize on it and go backwards and forwards until he wonders why he was ever worried. Don't make it a battle. Make it very easy for you both to succeed and then tell him he's a champion

and maybe give him a pick of grass or lead him home, just to let him know he's made a good decision.

If you need to lead a horse through any tricky area the worst thing you can do is pull on the reins of a snaffle bridle. As you pull forward the joint of the bit points into the roof of the horse's mouth, causing him to open his mouth and raise his head so he can't see down. If you are going out for training with an older horse, it is a good idea to fit a Dually halter or a headcollar underneath the bridle in case you need to lead your horse.

Before you attempt to go through water, make sure it is safe to cross. People throw all sorts of things in water, some of which you can't see. Ever since Pie got a shoe caught in an old wire mattress rusting on the bed of a river I've realized the importance of being cautious approaching water. He fell right down and as I held his head up above the water I thought he was going to drown. Thankfully, due in part to all our trust-building work together, he kept completely still as a passer-by managed to cut him loose with wire clippers. It was one of the most frightening experiences of my life.

> A great way to let your horse know he's done the right thing instantly is to jump off him there and then and lead him home – just try it a few times!

Going under low branches

When I entered my first Trec competition with Pie, I had no idea how low the obstacle was that you were meant to dip under. I walked the course the night before our first competition and saw the obstacle set up. It looked impossible! I had read that the height must be a minimum of 20 cm over the horse's withers but it hadn't really sunk in what a tiny space that was. To gain maximum points you are meant to canter under the gap. Yes, but how?

I got home that evening and decided that maybe Pie and I could do with a little practice at this. I am in no way biased but I can assure you Pie is a very intelligent horse. When I put a bamboo cane at the top of the jump wings and asked him to walk under it, he just thought 'better be careful here', reached up carefully with his nose and pushed it off before proceeding forward. What could I say? I felt a bit guilty because I wasn't totally happy with the exercise myself. Generally speaking, I'd much rather my horse stopped than carried me under low branches. Even when I led him under the bamboo pole, Pie reached up and

Opposite: 'The only place success comes before work is in the dictionary!'

Anon

Above: Introducing your horse to jumping a ditch – 'Coming together is a beginning. Keeping together is a progress. Working together is a success.'

Henry Ford

pushed it off to be on the safe side. Creative thinking was needed to encourage him to put his head down. It didn't take too much brainpower. He's been taught to lower his head to pressure but a bowl with his favourite food convinced him of the wisdom of moving through swiftly with his head down low and it soon became easy for him. Unfortunately, on the day, although Pie was perfect, we had a little trouble getting my er... 'derrière' under the pole!

Walking on a tarpaulin

Follow the basic safety rules. One way of getting your horse to touch the tarpaulin in a safe, stress-free way is for you to walk around the centre of it with the horse on the outside and he will gradually start to touch the edges and realize it doesn't bite. You could start with the tarpaulin very narrow and lead the horse over, although he may jump it to begin with. An ideal way to finish is with your horse standing quietly on the tarpaulin with no fuss. Make sure the tarpaulin is well secured at the edges so there is no chance of it suddenly blowing up or the horse tripping or catching on the edge.

PERFECT PARTNERS

Above: Jumping the ditch with the trained horse – 'The horses will leap over trenches, will jump out of them, will do anything else, providing one grants him praise and respite after his accomplishment.'

Xenophon

Left: Long lining over tarpaulin and tyres – 'The way of progress is neither swift nor easy.'

Marie Curie

Black plastic ditches – with herons in them

The fact that Daisy and Pie started to hit it off in 2003 meant that suddenly there was a whole new set of challenges. They had to move on from Novice to Open classes and the fences took on a much scarier dimension. In one of Pie's first Opens they were going really well until they were suddenly faced with a triple bar over a black plastic ditch. What happened next reminded me of what Monty sometimes says about the bad loaders he works with – 'He didn't say "no" he said "hell no"!'
Pie didn't stop at the fence. He stopped about 15 yards away when he first caught sight of it! On the second turn he gradually edged close enough to take a look but he was clearly not going to be jumping it that day. Daisy brought him out and said with honesty that she hadn't felt that keen on jumping it herself. Daisy doesn't carry a whip while riding Pie. The worst thing would have been to hit him that day – I was further convinced of this when I saw two separate incidents of ponies falling over in the class and seeing other riders falling off when their horses jumped erratically. At the risk of being repetitive I want to remind you: let's try and get our results as safely as possible.

So for Christmas, Daisy elected to have a black plastic water ditch for her main present (we do worry about her sometimes) and we started to practise. Something to be aware of is that although your horse may jump an obstacle at home, when he gets somewhere different he may well be frightened again when it's in a different setting. Plenty of people have set off confidently to their first show and then learned that little lesson! So, in my quest to be a good aunt, during Monty's February tour where Pie once again was making 'guest appearances', I packed up the black plastic water ditch and brought it out at every single venue. I'd pop Pie over it during our afternoon exercise.

By the end of the tour Pie had absolutely no fear of black plastic ditches and in March he was entered in his first Royal International qualifier. He was clear to the black plastic ditch and approaching it with absolute confidence when he suddenly noticed they'd put a stone heron in the ditch. He went on bravely but just lost his concentration and had the pole over the top down, otherwise jumping a clear round. Now why hadn't I ever thought of putting a heron in the ditch? Obviously, it was time for a visit to the garden centre!

Leading a horse over tarpaulin is an excellent way to develop the feel and timing that will be so beneficial in all your work with horses. If you feel your horse is abnormally frightened of the tarpaulin, to make things easier you could always lay the tarpaulin somewhere appropriate in his field and place his hay or some feed on it. Most horses soon come round to this and it's a gentle way of introducing something new, providing this method doesn't cause him to be deprived of food or water for any prolonged period of time or keep his anxiety levels up longer than is reasonable. Seeing other horses unconcerned is a good reassurance for your wary horse.

Jumping ditches

Make sure the ditch is safe, i.e. the banks are not going to give way, and your horse isn't going to run straight into a tree if he jumps too big. Start by leading him so he can have a good look at the ditch. When you feel ready to jump it, have a neck strap or hold some mane and sit firmly. You don't want to pull him in the mouth accidentally if he leaps a bit the first time (some horses have been told about crocodiles living in ditches).

'I have not failed. I have just found 10,000 ways that won't work.'

Thomas Edison

Long lining is also a good, safe way to introduce your horse to 'spooky' jumps such as ditches. Obviously there can be no jump wing on the side you are standing as the long lines would get caught in it. It means if he stops suddenly or gives an enormous leap, which horses often do on the first couple of tries at a new obstacle, there's no rider to pull him in the mouth or fall off. It gives the rider confidence as well to be sure the horse is capable of jumping the obstacle sensibly. If I'm going to long line a horse over a jump I prefer to use a Dually halter. Working with a roller as well gives more control. If a horse needed more impulsion I might use a plastic bag on a long bamboo cane for extra encouragement. Do remember though if the plastic bag has been used for desensitization that the horse won't naturally know he should move away from it!

Carrying flags or balloons

Flags can be bought from a fancy dress or party shop and fixed to your own desired lengths of bamboo cane. It's best to introduce your horse to the flags from the ground. Attach a rope to a Dually, hold it about two or three feet from his head and let him sniff the flag. Then gently stroke his body with it – if he moves away, stay nice and relaxed but do your best to keep the flag resting on him until he starts to settle down. Take the flag away as soon as he stands still and begins to relax. This action rewards him for relaxing and after a few minutes of repeating this and assessing how he is doing, you will be able gradually to work around his body so he is comfortable with the flag all over. Even if he kicks out with his back legs, keep the flag on his back until he settles down before removing it. This works equally well with a plastic bag on a bamboo stick. The method gradually gets a horse used to unusual stimuli.

When you first plan to ride with the flag, have someone pretend to pass it to you from the ground a few times to see how your horse reacts. Another good way of seeing how your horse is likely to react is to ride alongside someone carrying a flag on a trained horse. A round pen or small enclosed area is ideal for the early work.

Walking through flags

We had the idea to walk through flags with Pie midway through a tour with Monty and actually did the training as part of the demonstration. With Monty holding one large flag out and Recommended Associate Ian Vandenberghe standing opposite him holding out another, the idea was that I would ride Pie between them, pushing through the material and coming out the other side. Pie was understandably dubious about this at first. We gained his confidence by initially having Monty and Ian standing well apart so Pie could walk through a big gap with flags on

Left: Kelly and Pie at a demonstration at Berkshire College. Monty Roberts and Ian Vandenberghe are holding the flags.

either side (with lots of praise each time he came through the gap). Ian and Monty gradually closed the gap but it's not quite as simple as just making the gap smaller and smaller. If the horse starts to get concerned, it's important that your flag handlers discreetly make the gap that bit wider so he can manage easily. This has the psychological effect of making him braver, as he gets used to the flags opening for him and he comes through to lots of praise again, he wonders what he'd ever had doubts about. When Pie first went through the flags without the gap, he put his head down and pushed through, picking up pace, but once he realized that the flags weren't heavy (they were made of silk) or harmful in any way, he walked through easily, like an old pro.

When you see a horse coping so confidently, it's tempting to think there's nothing much to it anyway. However, all these little things you can teach your horse have the effect, if done correctly, of increasing the trust and understanding between the two of you as well as, very importantly, being fun!

> You don't want to mess up introducing your horse to scary obstacles but if it happens, you have to go as many steps backwards as necessary (figuratively not literally!) to regain your horse's confidence and gently start again. This also applies to jumping and similar situations, of course.

Traffic

Somebody came up to me at a demonstration once and said, 'Please reassure me that I'll be safe in traffic because I've followed some of your advice and my horse is fine now but I still have doubts.' What could I say? How on earth can I honestly say that someone is going to be safe in traffic? Some of the drivers around terrify me. It's not enough that they're travelling at 60 miles an hour on bendy country roads, but they're on their mobiles and eating a sandwich at the same time (I've really seen this!). The closest I ever came to being hit was by a woman driving a horsebox. Now if our own kind can't drive safely, how can we expect anyone else to? So let's reiterate the facts. Roads are extremely dangerous. Get a copy of the road safety rules from The British Horse Society. Make sure your knowledge of the Highway Code is up to scratch – get a copy from the Highways Agency. Don't take any silly chances.

On a more positive note, you can get your horse used to traffic so he is sensible if and when you decide to go near cars, lorries and bikes.

Above: Always make sure you can be seen in traffic and thank the drivers.

Horses that have problems with traffic have often been involved in some kind of accident or scare in the past, so step number one is to avoid those accidents and scares. The younger a horse is introduced to traffic the better. If a foal can see that his mother isn't scared by traffic around the place, that's an excellent start.

As we've already discussed, if something scares your horse it's much better to turn him towards it so that he can see it clearly. If there is a lorry trying to get past you on the road and your horse seems agitated, turn your horse back and walk past it, rather than letting it creep along in the horse's blindspot. Then turn around again as the lorry's going away. This gives your horse confidence, as if he has pushed the lorry away. Don't be afraid to give your horse lots of rubbing and stroking when he's worried but still holding himself together. I always did this with nervous racehorses, and successfully reassured and improved them. As I studied behaviourism more, I wondered, 'Have I been doing totally the wrong thing all along? Am I rewarding the horse for undesirable actions?' I decided to stay with what worked for me and analyse the theory later. In the case of giving your horse a stroke when he's frightened, it's not a situation of 'reward' but a time for reassurance.

Of course, if the rider is worried and upset as well, it could give a totally different message.

Ring of fire – *do* not *try this at home!*

When Monty and I were asked to work with the mounted police to train their horses to jump through tissue paper (now there's another whole chapter in itself!) I was excited at the prospect of seeing police horses work and how they are trained, but I did exact one favour – 'So long as I can bring Pie along and could I see how you jump through the ring of fire?' A big thank you to Inspector Alan Hiscox and the lovely Metropolitan policemen at Imber Court for setting this up for me.

I, like many others, had been brought up on *Black Beauty* and *Gone with the Wind* (Rhett Butler had to blindfold Scarlet's horse to get it out of the burning Atlanta) and believed that horses had an innate terror of fire. I've since learned, and this experience reinforced it for me, that horses actually aren't frightened of fire because they have no concept of what it is. They may well be frightened by the crackling sound of burning trees and, obviously, as soon as they feel burns they are going to go mad with pain and fear. However, fire on its own isn't a big deal. Even consciously knowing this and having a policeman with a blanket and fire extinguisher right there in case of something

---

Disregarding trains

'I must not forget to mention one part of my training, which I have always considered a very great advantage. My master sent me for a fortnight to a neighbouring farmer's, who had a meadow which was skirted on one side by the railway. Here were some sheep and cows, and I was turned in amongst them.

I shall never forget the first train that ran by. I was feeding quietly near the pales which separated the meadow from the railway, when I heard a strange sound in the distance, and before I knew whence it came – with a strange rush and clatter, and a puffing of smoke – a long black train of something flew by, and was gone almost before I could draw my breath. I turned, and galloped to the further side of the meadow as fast as I could go, and there I stood snorting with astonishment and fear. In the course of the day many other trains went by, some more slowly;

these drew up at the station close by, and sometimes made an awful shriek and groan before they stopped. I thought it very dreadful, but the cows went on eating very quietly, and hardly raised their heads as the black frightful thing came puffing and grinding past.

For the first few days I could not feed in peace; but as I found that this terrible creature never came into my field, or did me any harm, I began to disregard it, and very soon I cared as little about the passing of a train as the cows and sheep did.

Since then I have seen many horses much alarmed and restive at the sight or sound of a steam engine, but thanks to my master's good care, I am as fearless at railway stations as in my own stable.'

From Black Beauty *by Anna Sewell*

extraordinary happening, and even with Inspector Hiscox taking his good old horse over first, I must admit I felt odd as we built up to Pie and I jumping through the ring of fire. What fun! I rang my sister afterwards to tell her and she said, 'I don't believe it! Was he nervous about it?' I said, 'Well, his heart was pumping. I could feel the fear but I just carried him on anyway.' I confessed in the next sentence – actually, it was completely the other way round!

Smoke machine

One of my proudest moments with Pie! A police horse was meant to be giving us a lead past the smoke machine as we'd never seen one before. The police horse shied away from it and Pie carried on forward and gave him a lead! With a smoke machine one of the key things is the noise – it's apt to 'hiss' at odd intervals.

Another thing is the smell, and horses can be habituated to smell just as they can with everything else. Introduce them to things slowly to start with, i.e. don't expect/force them to get too close immediately, then gradually move in closer. Although Pie didn't have any particular issues with the smell, I wouldn't be averse to putting some food near the 'smelly' object to help your horse associate it with something pleasant.

See-saw

When Monty first mentioned using a 'teeter totter bridge', or see-saw, in a demonstration and described the height at which it should be balanced, at first I thought I'd misheard and then I thought perhaps he didn't understand English measurements properly. He had the measurements faxed over from America and I had a friend make it up accurately so we could show him he'd got it wrong. Admittedly, when I first saw it I thought it could be feasible but I didn't attempt it for some time. I was working hard on boosting Pie's confidence and had to be totally sure there wasn't going to be some mishap that would destroy all the trust we had built up.

Above: 'First ponder, then dare.'

Helmuth von Moltke

TEACHING YOUR HORSE TO BE BRAVE

I started his training with the see-saw by placing the board flat on the ground in the indoor school with the idea of just walking over it. Pie was having one of his 'Are you kidding or what?' moments. Ian Vandenberghe was there at the time and it's worth mentioning that he deliberately wandered off to concentrate on something else. Although you shouldn't worry about what other people are thinking, that's sometimes difficult with friends or colleagues – the rider's, or handler's, adrenalin levels go up, and the horse's adrenalin levels go up. One of Monty's favourite sayings is 'adrenalin up, learning down'. There's a lot to be said for just being left alone for a while to deal with things on your own, and yet it's also good to have someone close at hand who can help when appropriate. I suppose the key thing is to have the right person to help you.

In this case, when Pie stopped, I jumped off and led him over a couple of times. Then I got back on and rode him over, all very simple and stress free. There was no point in getting into a battle where one of us had to 'win'; when it's a partnership you know you're both on the

Below: Daisy riding Pie at the Royal Windsor Horse Show.

PERFECT PARTNERS

same side. I simply had to find a way to let him know it was safe and comfortable to do. Once Pie was completely calm about walking over the board, we worked on having him comfortable just standing quietly in the middle of the board. His learning to stand there quietly was an important step towards getting him to accept the 'teeter-totter' part. We started that on a low level before progressing to the full height.

The first time Monty saw us do the 'teeter-totter' exercise was during a demonstration in front of 1,000 people at Merrist Wood college. As I approached the obstacle it was strange because I was concentrating on the board and not looking at Monty, but out of the corner of my eye I could have sworn I saw him shaking his head and mouthing the words 'wrong way'. I dismissed it as my imagination playing tricks. Pie took the big step up, banged the board to the floor, teetered a few seconds and carried on over the board. Perfect! 'I'll be darned,' said Monty, going all American. 'I've never in my life seen a horse doing it that way round before. Didn't you know always to start from the low side?' Oops! Nobody had told me that! But then it's nice to think my little horse can show those American horses a thing or two!

Postscript to 'the Pie Plan'

On 17 July 2004 Daisy and Pie won at Kent County Show and qualified for the 'Working Hunter Pony of the Year'. When he got to the Horse of the Year Show he didn't knock the judges out with his beauty, but he did with his behaviour. He achieved equal top marks for manners and we were all very, very proud of him.

Above: 'Nothing else can quite substitute for a few well-chosen, well-timed, sincere words of praise. They're absolutely free – and worth a fortune.'

Sam Walton

Key points

- Actively work on this area of your horse's education.
- Make a plan – where are you now? Where do you want to be?
- Consider all the reasons why your horse is spooking – is he generally unconfident? Does he think he needs to protect you? Is it because of how he sees the object?
- Make sure your bond with your horse is good, make him feel

Above: Tackling the see-saw – 'Communicate as though all your goals depend on it – because they do!'

secure in your company, let him know you're reliable and trustworthy.

- Try gently desensitizing your horse to things with which he's not familiar.
- If you are in control of your horse's feet you will feel more confident and so will he!
- Anticipate your horse's reactions so you are prepared to react appropriately.
- When introducing your horse to new obstacles it is often better to start from the ground.
- Make a risk assessment and then ensure that you have the right equipment and a safe environment, and that everything is set up in your favour and your horse is schooled to an appropriate level.
- With moving scary objects, i.e. traffic, cows, prams etc., it gives the horse confidence if the horse follows the object as it moves away.
- Be flexible if plan A doesn't seem to be working. Never resort to anger or violence – that is not going to reassure your horse! Try different approaches such as having a lead horse, long lining or leading your horse yourself. Use your imagination and intelligence.

Fireworks and loud noises

Guy Fawkes' Night is a horrible time for many people as they worry about their animals. You have several options. If your horse is used to the radio during the daytime you can leave your radio playing in the evening to help disguise the sudden loud noises of the fireworks. Classical, particularly Baroque, music is perfect as it is shown in studies to have a mildly calming effect on horses. You could also consider desensitizing your horse to noise by the use of special 'Sounds of War' tapes, and there are even special tapes designed purely to help animals overcome their fear of fireworks. These are designed to be played quietly at the beginning of the animal's training and then you build up the volume. Dog owners will know how dogs can pick up concern from their owners and when you hear fireworks it's best to say, 'Isn't this exciting!' My horses are stabled at night and appear unconcerned by fireworks, but I get really annoyed that people let them off in an area so populated by horses.

I'm sure to take a few deep breaths before I go over to the stables. After all, if I were to go over to the horses seething with anger, how are they meant to know it's not directed at them?

Some horses hate the sound of clippers, maybe because of a bad experience or perhaps they're just not used to the noise. It's a good idea to desensitize your horse to the noise and feel of a hairdryer before introducing the clippers. He'll grow to enjoy the feeling of the warm air, particularly if he's cold or wet. It may take minutes or weeks, but carry on until he's totally happy to accept the air blown over him. When it's time to introduce the clippers, keep the hairdryer on, and stroke him with the clippers turned off at the same time. Once he accepts that, work with the hairdryer on and the clippers on. The two sets of noise baffles even the most hardened clipper hater to accept them peacefully. Eventually, you'll be able to turn the hairdryer off and take it away altogether.

How to have a horse that loves going places with you

Going out for rides should be a joy for horse and rider, so it's a pity when you get to hear about a nappy horse. The Americans call a horse like this 'barn sour' or a 'balker' or 'jibber'. This is generally a horse that doesn't want to be ridden away from his stable or field or from anywhere his friends are. He may suddenly stop on a ride and refuse to go forward, or he may rear and whip round in order to face home. The main thing to appreciate is that not only is it not much fun but it means the horse isn't having much fun either.

Possible reasons for nappiness

- The horse has physical problems, such as soreness or discomfort. Your vet should give him a complete check over and recommend a physiotherapist/chiropractor/oesteopath if there are back problems. His teeth and mouth should be inspected. If none of these professionals can find anything wrong but the horse still seems depressed, ask the vet to take a blood test and check for viruses or worm damage.
- The equipment used on the horse is causing him discomfort. Check that the saddle is fitting correctly and that the bit is comfortable in his mouth. If you are using a martingale, or any other equipment, check that it isn't too tight – and check that it's necessary to use it at all.
- The general management of the horse is not good, i.e. the horse is overfed and underexercised or underfed and overexercised. He is bored and frustrated generally with his routine.

Two Americans were talking about their ranches. The first one brags, 'Why, my ranch is so big if I start off riding at 6 o'clock in the morning, I still haven't got to the other side by 10 o'clock that night.' The other rancher replies, 'Yeah, I once had a horse like that.'

Opposite: 'We're not lost: we're locationally challenged!'

- The horse has never been taught to understand the aids in the first place. He is too 'green' and insecure to be going out on his own.
- The horse was pushed into going out on his own before he was ready and has grown up to develop napping as a normal part of his routine.

- The horse has never been taught rein back as a natural aid by the rider and discovering it for himself thinks, 'Ah-ha! Now I've found something she can't handle!'
- The rider always rides briskly back to the stables and gets off there.
- The horse has overbonded with another horse.
- The horse is ridden very rarely and can think of no reason why he should suddenly go off to a strange place and leave all his friends.
- The horse has played around on the roads a little. The rider is worried about the horse slipping (with good reason) and tends to 'freeze'. The horse is aware of this and feels empowered by it.
- The rider always rides the horse right back to the stable/field where he is fed, rested and watered. This makes the stable/field the one and only comfort zone.
- The horse has been frightened or overworked on a ride. I've found this particularly with racehorses that have been made to gallop up steep hills before they are ready, or had a very hard race, and it completely disheartens them for the future.
- The horse has been whipped for hesitating and has now got very resentful of being ridden and backs up into any pressure as soon as he perceives he's being threatened.
- Racehorses that run away often nap before they get on the gallops as well. They frighten themselves by bolting but don't know any alternative, so they don't want to go on to the gallop.
- The horse has been over-restricted and constantly forced into an outline. When this happens you will often get a horse that takes his rider by surprise by suddenly reacting because he needs to let

his tired muscles rest. Dutch Olympic Gold medalist, Anky van Grunsven, constantly stresses the need for dressage horses to be rewarded with a stretch and loose work.

- The rider is insecure or nervous. She may be inconsistent with her aids, pushing him forward one moment, pulling him back the next, so he has learned to nap in the general confusion.
- The horse may have had a weak rider in the past and consequently has no faith in any rider now.
- After following the same route every day, the horse is asked to go a different way. The horse, being a creature that can develop habits quickly, thinks, 'Hey, you've made a mistake here!'

Above: 'We have all the time in the world to get things right. But it only takes a short time to get things horribly wrong!'

Anon

Making a bad situation worse

- The horse has stopped because he is very frightened. His heart is beating fast but the rider ignores this and thumps the horse with her legs. The fear and adrenalin take the horse back to his natural instincts, i.e. back into the pressure, so he starts moving backwards. The horse is not 'napping' at all. He is scared of something and wants to have a look. This is normal behaviour and giving the horse some time to process what he is seeing will help him become bolder and braver in the future.

- The horse has napped a little and been bullied or punished severely, making him confused and resentful and determined to 'fight for his rights' at every opportunity, even if he has a nice rider now.

- The rider, without being an overtly 'bad' horsewoman, has a lot of doubts about her riding, or life in general, and this is transmitted to the horse. Her horse is, in effect, protecting her from doing too much. Something along these lines has been in horse folklore for years and I admit I had some resistance to it. I favoured more prosaic explanations for a horse's behaviour, such as, 'The rider's holding the horse too tight.' However, with experience, I now believe that in some cases where a good bond exists between horse and rider, the horse is not being disobedient when he won't go on the road or over a jump. He is stopping because he has picked up from the rider that she feels the course of action is dangerous and he is protecting her. The first step is for the rider to acknowledge this and take responsibility. Then it may be possible for her to change her actions as well as her attitude to help her horse.

> 'Every time you ride, you are teaching or unteaching your horse.'
>
> **Gordon Wright**

What you can do

Prevention

First of all, look at all the aforementioned causes and check if anything can be remedied before you start any retraining.

If you have a young horse that is still learning the aids, work in an enclosed area and have an older horse go in front of him until he gains confidence. To build his self-esteem and confidence, avoid testing him too much in the early stages. Put him in situations where he can receive lots of praise for being such a brave, good horse. Make sure he has the right amount of exercise for his age – he must not be pushed to go on until he is tired and sore. He should be happy with you touching him all over and maintain a respectful distance from you unless invited to come closer. You should be able to control all his movements – forwards, backwards, sideways and standing still – both on the ground and from the saddle.

Use a loose style of riding

There is a style that works very well on the reluctant horse – you will see the successful rider in a very 'loose' style of riding. They will have longer reins freely given to the horse or they might ride with their hands deliberately forward to be absolutely sure the horse's head is completely free, although they can bring their hands back quickly to regain contact if they feel the need. They will often tend to use one leg at a time to encourage the horse forward rather than both legs. They may move each leg backwards and forwards independently to encourage the horse forward. The rider may keep changing the horse's direction so he may not be going straight but at least he is going forward and giving some movement. Experienced riders of young horses will often use this style until the horse is ready to go in a more collected fashion.

Get off

I used to think if you got off a napping horse or a horse that refused to go past something, it was 'giving in' and then he 'would know he had won' – put in inverted commas for all those who know that old-school style of thinking. In practice, I found that horses were usually

---

CASE STUDY

Be honest with yourself

A lady came to me because she felt her horse was nappy and also, when they went out hunting, he was stopping at obstacles that he was easily capable of jumping. I only had to listen to her for a very short time to realize that she was terrified of hunting and didn't really want to go at all. It was very likely the horse believed he was protecting her. We did various exercises to build up her confidence and, starting with gridwork, went on to tackle individual fences, which they jumped well. This was just in one lesson as she lived some distance away. I heard that things were going well but after a month or so I had another phone call from her. The horse had stopped at a fence on the hunt and her husband was very angry that she hadn't kept up. He had suggested that she get in touch with me to suggest some 'stronger methods' she could use to make sure this didn't happen again. I said I couldn't help in that direction because I didn't think it would be fair on her or the horse. She actually agreed with this and we discussed the idea that she really needed to talk with her husband about her true feelings about riding and what it was she wanted to do and felt happy doing.

A HORSE THAT LOVES GOING PLACES

Above: 'You're not obligated to win. You're obligated to do the best you can every day.'
Marian Wright Edelman

genuinely nervous or unsure and getting off could solve the problem without making a big deal of it. Gradually the horse would overcome his fears.

Having a lead horse for a while, or someone to lead your horse from the ground while you're in the saddle, can help overcome the situation, too. There comes a point when you expect your horse to go anywhere and walk past anything, but that's a result of correct training and not a right you have. Do give young horses time to develop and gain confidence. Pushing them to do too much before they are ready will do more harm than good.

Get your horse excited about going out

Horses are social animals. They love to be part of the crowd, doing what their pals are doing. You don't see herds galloping around with one or two standing to the side as if saying, 'I really can't be bothered today.' If you'd like your horse to enjoy galloping around the countryside, it could be a great idea to join other horses galloping around the countryside in a drag hunt. If you'd prefer something a little more sedate, some type of organized ride may be ideal. You could even organize a sponsored ride yourself in aid of a worthwhile charity.

Tactics that can help in emergency situations

There's no advantage in turning a situation into a big battle with you and your horse on opposite sides. Keep a sense of humour and remember that you are going to get to where you want to be in the end. The horse simply doesn't understand what's the best thing to do and it's up to you to persuade him that your way is the best way. Of course, you must be sure that it is. If he's behaving completely out of character, make sure he's not just protecting you from something.

> The French have a saying that translates 'leg without hand, hand without leg'. If you applied it to your car it would mean 'don't keep braking and accelerating at the same time'.

- Rein back. You have already schooled your horse to back up well (yes you have!) so he is not able to use this as a tactic against you. Curiously, if a horse is frightened or suspicious of something, while he may not go past it forwards, he will often go past it backwards – a useful ploy.
- Circle him. Another useful tactic for a frequent napper is to let him know it will mean more work for him by circling him five or so times in each direction, pausing for a second and then giving him the option to go forward again. If he refuses, circle again.
- Shake the reins on his neck. Have the reins very loose so there is no chance of pulling on his mouth, and shake or slap them on alternate sides of his neck. I call this the 'Newmarket' method

because many of the racing lads prefer this tactic, even though they carry whips. You may have seen photographs of racing lads with their hands forward and to one side or the other, or just gently encouraging a horse forward by shaking the reins.

Get off your butt!

This is one of the best pieces of advice in the whole book so don't miss it!

When I first started riding, and especially in racing, we were always told to get off the horse, loosen his girth and walk the last half-mile home. The reason for this was partly to be sure that the horse was relaxed and cool when he got back to the stable, but it had major psychological benefits as well. Is it a coincidence that I don't remember any nappy horses from those times? Think about it. If the stable/field is the source of everything good, i.e. food, water, companionship, rest, it is obvious the horse is going to be strongly drawn to that area.

It's far better for the horse never to know quite when he is going to get the bonus of the rider getting off. Time it so that when the horse does something particularly well, e.g. performs a good move in a schooling session, jump off at that moment and praise him effusively. Let the deal be it is the good move that gets him the rest, not getting to the stables. I've found jumping off is such a successful reinforcer, I want you to try it. So if you have your own horse, please humour me. Think of something you'd really like him to get enthusiastic about – backing up? Jumping? Standing in a nice outline? Going into the ménage? For two weeks, every single time you exercise your horse, finish with that particular action and jump off. Then email me and tell me you can't believe how well it works!

The Giddy-up rope

Use of the Giddy-up, also known as the 'Wip Wop', can sometimes be appropriate to improve the forward movement of a reluctant horse. It's made from soft rope and does not inflict any pain on the horse. If using pain got horses to go forward, there would be absolutely no nappy

---

Listen to your horse

27 December 2004. On a clear, cold day my niece Daisy takes Floyd for a ride around the village. 'You'll never guess what happened,' she says when she gets back. 'He suddenly stopped and wouldn't go forward. I thought, "How weird," so I got off to lead him forward and the road was completely like ice. I couldn't see it at all from on top of him. Thank goodness he stopped!'

Opposite: 'People are always good company when they are doing what they really enjoy.'
Samuel Butler

horses in the world. It's a fact. I would think that 99 per cent of the nappy horses that come to us for retraining have been hit to try to make them go forward and it hasn't worked.

Where a whip hits a horse solidly, the horse will often move into the pressure. It will often cause him to be resentful or frightened, neither of which are helpful. The Giddy-up has a light, ticklish action that you use behind your leg. Sometimes the noise and motion from hitting your own leg with it is enough to encourage forward motion.

Fear is not 'resistance' – fear is fear

If the horse's heart is beating very fast, that is not napping, that is fear. Let him settle down completely before you think about using the Giddy-up or your legs. If you put pressure on a frightened horse, he may react with panic, whipping round, rearing, backing into the pressure. One of the aims of an intelligent horseperson should be to live a long time, so just sit quietly for a minute. Once the horse has got over his fear, it may not be necessary to use anything at all and you can just proceed forwards calmly.

How to use the Giddy-up

The principle works when a horse is unwilling to go forward. Make sure your hands are very giving with the reins, perhaps hold your hands forward, and be sure that you are not accidentally preventing any forward movement. As usual, check that the facilities are safe. Ideally, use an enclosed area with a non-slip surface and introduce the equipment gradually.

Place your hand through the loop and hold the top of the rope. Let it hang down by your side and then bring your hand up, swinging the rope in front of you and through to the opposite side so that it touches the horse just behind your leg. Swing it back so that it touches the horse just behind your leg on the first side and repeat until the horse goes forward. The movement should be fluid. At the same time, you could try applying and slackening pressure with your legs in a loose, rhythmic bumping effect. Once the horse goes forward, stop instantly as a reward.

Opposite: 'We are all travelers in the wilderness of this world, and the best we can find in our travels is an honest friend.'
Robert Louis Stevenson

A HORSE THAT LOVES GOING PLACES

The Giddy-up can be used as a visual aid, which is why we have them made in white. Sometimes, allowing a young horse to see one out of the corner of his eye may be enough to achieve some forward movement. Also, the noise it makes as you hit your leg or boot with it, for instance, can be used as an energiser.

If you are not finding any success with this method, do ask a more experienced rider for help and advice. You may be doing something unhelpful that you are not aware of.

In a couple of extreme cases, both racehorses, I found having the horse in blinkers did the trick. Once the horse was going freely, the blinkers could come off. If you feel blinkers are a bit 'over the top' you might like to consider using sheepskin covers on the cheekpieces of your horse's bridle which also restrict some backward vision but in a rather more subtle way.

'The weekend cure'

The first weekend course I ever ran, in 1996, was a 'Nappy Horse Clinic'. I had a clear plan of how I was going to run the weekend, but the nearer the time came, the more doubts I had about whether I had bitten off more than I could chew. I was even more anxious after I spoke

---

Trust goes both ways

'There he is,' said the dealer as he hopped over the gate with a rope and clipped it on to the four-year-old chestnut Arab gelding's headcollar. He leapt on to the horse's back and raced round the field. Then he rode him back to the gate and said, 'Here he is, one hundred and fifty quid and I'll deliver him.' I was a total greenhorn in my early twenties (it was a long time ago) and Rengo was to be my first horse.

A very muddy horse arrived the following week. 'He likes to roll,' the dealer said before leaving very quickly with my cash. I had the stable all ready for him and proceeded to lead this very nervous Arab inside where I started to feed him and clean him up. Underneath all the mud were hardened scabs of rain scald so riding was out while I treated his back. This took a month but I was so keen to work with him that we went running every morning at 6.00 a.m. before work. If Rengo was walking by the time I got home, I was doing well. When he got nervous I would just talk quietly to him and stroke him. Gradually I thought we were getting to know each other. The time came to ride. By now his coat was shining like copper and he was bursting with energy – maybe just a bit too much. Rengo was far smarter than I realized. We became best friends and I rode him every day but there were some places Rengo wouldn't go no matter how hard I tried, so we stuck to parts of the mountain we knew. It turned out for the best because some months later a neighbour riding in the same area got stuck in a bog with his stallion. Later he told me he thought the horse was playing up so rode forcefully. It took him three hours to get his exhausted horse out and, yes you guessed it, that was one of the places where Rengo wouldn't go. I often think about my time with Rengo, how we were a good team, how much he taught me and looked after me while, at the time, I thought I was teaching and looking after him.

Recommended Associate John Jones

with my mentor, Monty Roberts, who said, 'You're going to run your first clinic for five nappy horses and their riders? You must be crazy!'

In fact, looking back, there is very little I would change. I was lucky enough to have obtained outstanding facilities for the weekend. Not only did we have the use of a very large indoor school and an outdoor school, but we could also go through a farmyard area with tractors and machinery and there was a zoo on the premises. We could walk past llamas, emus and the most delightful tapir, and then on through some woods and back home again. When I say outstanding facilities, I mean outstanding!

Here's what happened on the weekend.

- All horses were verified sound before they came to the clinic.
- One fewer horse turned up than was booked – the owner couldn't load him in the horsebox. This is significant because it's clear now that the two problems often go together, i.e. the owner isn't able to control the horse's movement on any level. In fact, we had three horses and one miniature spotted pony that was napping when he was being driven. During the course of the weekend, I actually worked with all three of the horses to get them to load better, as they each had mild to quite severe problems with this.

> 'The problem is not that there are problems. The problem is expecting otherwise and thinking that having problems is a problem.'
>
> **Theodore Rubin**

- To begin with, I talked through what we were going to do during the weekend and the theory behind it. We discussed and checked saddles, bits and any other equipment.
- After instruction, each owner did a Join Up with her horse to nurture a bond of trust and respect.
- Each owner did basic work with her horse on a training halter, again to increase trust and respect.
- Each owner led her horse over a piece of tarpaulin – starting to test the trust now!
- Each owner long lined her horse around the indoor school and over poles and then over the tarpaulin. This was to increase the horse's confidence and responses without having someone at his head.
- Each owner then long lined her horse around the property, successfully passing the llamas, emus and the delightful tapir. This tested the trust again.

'Always know
the direction
of true north.'

PERFECT PARTNERS

A HORSE THAT LOVES GOING PLACES

- Each owner did some ridden work in the indoor school. We looked at various ways the riders could encourage their horses to go forward more happily.
- By now, rider confidence was improving and they knew that they would be successful – a very important point.
- One rider had problems with her horse stopping at jumps, so I got her doing some gridwork with her horse, gradually building the jumps up a little higher so they both gained confidence.
- Nobody was allowed – well, nobody actually asked – to carry a whip all weekend. We showed a couple of them how to use a Giddy-up rope, but as it happened, nobody had cause to use it.
- At the end of the weekend, all the horses were ridden individually by their owners around the property and past the llamas, emus and the delightful tapir. SUCCESS!

Key points

- Try to discover why your horse doesn't want to go out for rides. Look through the list of possible causes carefully and see if any of them apply.
- If you are the rider it's essential you look at yourself honestly – are you confident and happy taking your horse on rides?
- Prevention is always easier than cure. Try to ensure the training of your young/green horse is not frightening for him and don't do too much with him before he's ready. Keep aiming for a keen, confident partner.
- Make sure you're riding safely and effectively and are not impeding the horse's forward movement by holding his head in too tightly.
- It is not defeat to get off and lead, or to be led by another person or horse, in a tricky situation. It can be a useful tactic.
- Time your dismount so that it works in your favour.
- Always have back-up plans ready to try in an emergency, e.g. backing the horse past something or circling.
- Remember you and your horse are on the same side. Work out ways to make it a pleasure for him to go out for rides.

Opposite: 'To get where you want to go you must keep on keeping on.'
Norman Vincent Peale

Horses behaving badly – bucking and bolting and rearing (oh my!)

8

Each challenge in this chapter can range from being a little worrying to extremely dangerous and they can move from one level to another amazingly quickly. Do not try to tackle any of these problems without the help of a very experienced person unless you are extremely experienced yourself. Even then, make sure you have someone present who could call an ambulance if necessary. That isn't a sign of being nervous or scaremongering – it's merely common sense.

As with any problem, first of all you've got to find out why the horse thinks this unwanted behaviour is a good idea. Once you've found that out, you never know, you might just find that you agree with him.

Bucking

There are several reasons why a horse may buck:

- He is in physical discomfort, particularly with something pinching in his back.
- He has a memory of past discomfort.
- He is in physical discomfort from the saddle.
- The rider can't sit in the saddle comfortably.
- The rider is too heavy, sits too far back, is lopsided, or is unstable.
- He was not started properly in the first place and has a big fear of being ridden.
- The rider gets on one day wearing a brand new bright yellow raincoat that makes crinkly noises. (I've done this one!)
- He isn't used to wearing an exercise sheet and on a windy day it starts blowing around.

'Deep thoughts: if you're a horse, and someone gets on you, and falls off, and then gets right back on you, I think you should buck him off again right away.'

Saturday Night Live (satirical US TV show)

Opposite: 'Riding: "The art of keeping a horse between you and the ground."'

Anon

- He has bucked people off a few times and now it seems like a good thing to do, i.e. he's been trained to do it.
- He is overfresh on a particular day, or in general, and, as Jamie Oliver would say, is just 'having a laugh'.

Horses that buck seriously often end up with a one-way ticket somewhere and I'm not talking 'good home' here. If you have a horse that bucks and you want to stop him doing it, it's up to you to get to the root of the cause. If you can't, the sensible course of action is to bring in someone with more experience. Make your first responsibility to do the best you can for this horse. Trying to prove you can do it all yourself is just ego.

If you can look at the situation as a challenge, you'll find that far more helpful than regarding it as some great disaster. Students have said to me that having a problem with a horse caused them to look at horses and horsemanship in a whole different light. Some have even said it was the best thing that ever happened to them.

'Problems are a major part of life. Don't whinge about why you always have problems...get on with solving them. Take it from someone who has been there – the solving gets easier as you go along.'

Sara Henderson,
1936 Australian Outback
station manager and writer

He is in physical discomfort

Try to assess if there is obvious unsoundness, especially with his back. It's good to develop an eye and a feeling for these things. The next step, whether you're sure you've found something or not, is to get in touch with a good equine vet who can help or recommend the services of a good physiotherapist, osteopath, chiropractor, acupuncturist or whichever practitioner he feels is most appropriate.

Remember, however, that these physical tests may represent a 'snapshot' of your horse's state at that particular moment. Intermittent pain can be very difficult to spot. It may be necessary to repeat the checks. If you feel you have evidence of physical discomfort or gait irregularity, it may be a good idea to video the horse to show the vet or practitioner that you aren't imagining the whole thing. It may even be that your horse needs X-rays to explore the possibility of spinal disease.

Make other welfare checks, too, such as sending off for a worm count and a blood test, and do make sure that you are having your horse's teeth checked by a good equine dental technician regularly. If your horse is female, ask the vet to check for ovarian or

Left: A good horse trainer can hear a horse talk, a great trainer can hear him whisper, but Yorkshire lass Sarah Dent likes things spelt out for her in good old-fashioned English!

reproductive abnormalities as well. I'm sure nobody's ever suggested to you that keeping a horse is cheap! You've just got to keep on top of these things in general. I know caring, loving horse owners who have been shocked at the results of random tests – and that includes me.

He has a memory of past discomfort
This is so tricky to deal with. Once you've put the horse through every physical test known to man or beast and it is absolutely certain that his behaviour problems are not pain-related but he is still showing signs to suggest they are, what do you do? If you are totally and absolutely sure that the chance of it being real pain is non-existent, the only possible solution is a complete restarting programme aimed at re-establishing trust and building confidence.

Remember, all training starts from the ground. Does your horse lead respectfully, back up, and move from side to side easily in hand? Are you able to touch him all over and handle every area, even the areas where there was pain at one stage? If not, it's not going to get any easier once you are on top of the horse. Putting him through mental discipline will help him to control his nerves. You can't expect a horse not to be frightened but you can expect him to control his fear. Just think of how fabulous many police horses are through good training and discipline without harshness.

This is an ideal time to work through a range of physical and rehabilitation exercises with your horse. I particularly like those developed

Keep your horse in good shape

As with humans, horses need to have a balanced body to enable them to move well and without discomfort. If the muscles are not working in harmony, their actions against the bone levers can be badly affected, which means the horse's balance and posture will be badly affected and this will be seen in the strange way his muscles develop. In the long term, it will cause the horse pain and discomfort and this regularly leads to behavioural problems and loss of performance. All you need to know about a horse's performance ability, posture and balance is written all over him in terms of his muscle development – it's just another language you need to learn how to read.

Take a close look at the horse in the picture opposite. See how the muscles in his forehand – the pectorals, triceps and all the muscles around the shoulder – are large and overdeveloped but along the back and over the quarters there is hardly any muscle at all. The chestnut horse, opposite, is telling you that he cannot work through from behind and is forced to pull himself along from the front. Because of this, the muscles that push the horse

along from the back have withered away and the muscles that pull him along from the front have been worked so hard that they are massively overdeveloped. This is effectively two horses joined in the middle and his musculo-skeletal balance and posture have been badly affected, leading to pain through his back and neck and plummeting performance ability. It has taken this horse a long time to get into this poor state and it will take a lot of remedial work and physiotherapy to get him back to the condition he needs to be in to move comfortably.

So take a good look at your horse. Are his muscles in balance? Look at the front half of his body and then look at the back half. Do they look as if they belong to the same horse? Also look at your horse from behind. Do his hip joints look level? Is the muscle development the same on each side? If not, find a good physiotherapist who can help get your horse back in shape. Remember, your horse is relying on you.

Dr Gail Williams BA (Hons), PhD

Left: Chestnut horse with muscle wastage.

Opposite and below: Pie enjoying his treatments!

by Mary Bromiley and Linda Tellington-Jones (books and courses are available by both these practitioners). Long lining is another good exercise to practise but don't forget that the more tense the horse is, the more he feels pain. The more frightened he is, the more likely he is to perceive that he is feeling pain even though what you are doing wouldn't affect another horse in the same physical condition.

Conversely, adrenalin can sometimes make the horse less sensitive to pain – as in the horse that resents schooling but is willing at shows or out on hacks. (See 'Discomfort from the saddle', below.) People often deduce that if the horse behaves well in one situation, he must be 'having you on' when he's difficult in another, but this isn't necessarily the case. Racehorses and human athletes have been known to race, and even win, with bone fractures. A Californian report on post mortems on 36 racehorses found that nearly 50 per cent had incomplete lumbar vertebral fractures and 25 per cent had incomplete pelvic fractures. Even many of us non-athletes know the feeling of complete recovery from exhaustion or minor ailments if the right offer comes up.

A horse that has ever received electric shock treatments in his 'training' is one of the most difficult and sometimes dangerous to help because of his fear and anticipation of what's going to happen. In this case, it can take a great deal of time to re-establish trust.

He is in physical discomfort from the saddle

At demonstrations, after examining the horse, the first thing we do with 'incurable buckers' is check the saddle. In an amazing number of cases once the saddle is put right the horse is miraculously cured. One horse was going to be sold because she was 'nappy when going out' even though she was 'great at shows'. We looked at her saddle and found three staples sticking out of the flocking and into her back. Corresponding lumps had developed, like large insect bites, where they had been digging into her. The saddle also had a twisted gullet.

Saddles can be asymmetrical, have lumpy flocking or be too tight or too loose on the horse, and that's just a start! If the saddle is too long, it is positively inviting the horse to buck because it will press on the sensitive area of the back. It mustn't be placed over the horse's shoulder, either. The saddle must be placed in the right position to be comfortable for the horse. As a top saddler furiously pointed out, 'Some of the ways these saddles are slapped on – these women wouldn't stick a bra on round their waist and expect it to do any good!'

Uncomfortable girths can cause bucking as well, particularly when pulled up tightly too quickly. Another potential aggravation to look out for is a 'balance strap' at the back of the girth straps, or a point strap at the front. These can pull the saddle into an unnatural position, which can cause discomfort and resentment, as can metal buckles sticking into the horse's sides.

The rider can't sit in the saddle comfortably
This one's easier to spot! Have you ever been asked to sit on an unruly show pony and tried to ride it in a pony show saddle – it feels dreadful and doesn't do justice to your riding or to the pony. Personally, I prefer a more general purpose or showjumping-style saddle with a flatter seat. Of course, the horse's comfort has top priority but your own safety and comfort has got to be near the top of the list as well. When choosing the perfect saddle for your horse, discuss what is best for both the horse and for you with the fitter.

The rider is too heavy, sits too far back, is lopsided, is unstable
This rider makes it uncomfortable for the horse to be ridden. Don't worry – if you have studied Chapter 4, 'Please Ride Properly', this won't be you! If Olympic riders are still taking lessons, so can the rest of us. If you are not already doing so, find a good instructor who will assess your riding position. You may find it helpful to be videoed to see if you can spot any imperfections for yourself. Continually to search for improvement is part of the fun of horsemanship. If you find something that needs improving – celebrate!

> 'We learn wisdom from failure much more than success. We often discover what we will do by finding out what we will not do.'
>
> Samuel Smiles,
> Scottish author and
> social reformer

He was not started properly in the first place and has a big fear of being ridden
Surprisingly common, this often happens with particularly good-natured horses. He may have been taken for granted in the early stages and not introduced to what was expected of him respectfully and in a methodical fashion. When, through lack of education and care, the horse takes fright at something and throws someone off, he's turned out for a few months to 'see if that helps'. While that course of action certainly helps viral diseases and stress in horses, I have never known

it help a case like this without additional attention. It is perfectly natural for a horse in fear to go back to his basic instinct of 'getting that predator off his back' if his confidence and trust haven't been built up. This horse is similar to one with a memory of past discomfort. His whole education has to be started again from the ground and continued in the saddle. This time, no stone should be left unturned in developing his confidence in humans and life in general.

He has bucked people off a few times and now it seems like a good thing to do, i.e. he's been trained to do it
This is the serious bucker, the type that plunges with his head between his legs, possibly twisting his whole body in his effort to get the rider off his back. While this behaviour is often described as 'nasty', the nasty part lies in the injuries the rider can sustain. The horse is just being a horse, doing what he thinks is the right thing. If he was a rodeo horse in America, he would be positively applauded for his behaviour and told he was a great horse. Never underestimate how much we can lead horses into behaving in a particular way. All the time you are with your horse you are training him, whether you mean to be or not. For the horse that has found instant reward by getting people off his back, the habit can become ingrained and hard for the average rider to deal with – maybe any rider.

This may be one of the very few times when I might consider using the piece of equipment Monty calls the 'buck stopper'. With this, the horse teaches himself that it's uncomfortable to throw his head down and buck in such a way as to dislodge the rider. The principle is similar to the 'grass reins' that are occasionally used on children's ponies to stop them putting their heads down to eat grass any time they feel like it. The grass reins run from the D rings of the saddle, through the sides of the browband and on to the bit. They prevent the pony putting his head down and possibly pulling the child over his neck at the same time, and make riding safer and more enjoyable for the child. It may be better for a small adult to re-school the pony, though. Children are meant to have ponies for fun and being terrorized isn't fun.

The buck stopper is generally made of cord – the sort you might use to adjust blinds up and down, but not too thin. The cord is anchored firmly around the saddle and then goes up the neck and is fitted over the poll, down each side of the horse's face and under his top lip, above the teeth. It has no effect at all unless the horse swings his head down sharply. Many horses learn very quickly when fitted with a buck stopper but they must be checked for pain and other problems first. It would be totally unethical to use it on a horse that had something wrong with him.

I don't encourage or recommend people to use this equipment. It's much better to explore the other options fully. I have used it in demonstrations – mostly when I'm told that it's the horse's last chance somehow to be made rideable. A horse that is capable of seriously injuring people is often heading to be put down if nothing can be done. There have been some excellent successes with this method but the owner has to have the time, talent and nerve to carry on with the horse in the same manner after the demonstration or training to ensure permanent success. I am lucky enough at the present time to work with specialist riders, Grant Bazin and Dan Wilson. They are seriously good riders of horses that want to get you off. Even though they have the option to be 'rough riders' if they want to be, their whole attitude and philosophy is the same as the rest of the team's – try to understand the horse's point of view before anything else. Loving and caring about horses is no longer girly stuff!

It's worth remembering that it takes a big effort for a horse to buck. Those valuable rodeo horses are expected to buck for seconds only before they are rewarded with a break. If they went on for too long or did it too regularly, they would soon lose the urge to expend so much effort. Horses have had to develop quick learning abilities to survive in the wild. If an easier option is given to them, they can unlearn past bad habits.

He is overfresh on a particular day
Here you have a horse that likes to try out a buck or two every now and then. You'll have made all the checks but perhaps occasionally when you get on you feel him like 'a coiled spring' and, assuming you're not a Grant or Dan, you start to think, 'Uh-oh, I could be in trouble here.' If you don't want to get straight on, consider long lining in circles until he settles down.

If you find this is a regular occurrence, I would advise you to think about how much you're feeding your horse in relation to the exercise

Above: 'I don't like horses: both ends are dangerous, and the middle bit's uncomfortable.'

Anon

he's getting and turn-out time. Competition horses are most liable to these bursts of overexcitement but the experienced competition rider can generally cope easily. The ones who can't cope are the children who are expected to ride hyped-up show ponies while simultaneously trying to keep their fixed smiles in place for the judge. You often see ponies being led or lunged for hours before classes and I can't deny that both of these strategies may have their place in those circumstances. However, let me give you some tips for getting on a regular horse that you can feel has his back up a bit.

Have a bridge in your reins, like the racing riders do. Holding the reins together like this prevents the horse pulling you forward because the bridge will push on to his withers and you can push yourself back. You may like to ride with your legs a little further forward and your stirrups a bit shorter than usual, and be sure to keep sitting up.

A horse that is going to give a few bucks in this overfresh fashion usually gives plenty of warning. You can feel his back come up and if he's going to give a proper buck, he's going to have to put his head down.

The worst thing is just to be given a leg-up and then launch off into the distance – this is positively encouraging the horse to go into a bronco act. Riding him in tight circles is a good idea. If you've been to one of Monty's or my demonstrations, you'll know that with a rider on a first-time starter we keep the horse moving in very small circles around ourselves – a horse finds it very hard to buck if he's got his head bent round. If you're trying this with your overfresh horse, do it in a soft, safe, enclosed area. You could have someone hold the horse to start with to keep him in small circles but after that continue the circles yourself. Be prepared to lift your hands immediately if you feel his head attempt to go down. By lifting your hands, you lift his head, again preventing him putting his head down.

Timing

One of the trickiest times to prevent bucking is just after a horse has jumped. You must have a really secure seat and be ready to raise your hands after each jump, but don't discount the previous advice about saddles and physical checks because it could easily be something pinching that encourages the horse to do this.

Hitting a horse when he bucks is one of the worst things you can do, yet is one of the most common. It doesn't make him 'know he's doing wrong', it just makes him kick out in irritation and want to get you off even more! What can work well as a 'penalty' is pulling him up and circling him in each direction a few times before pushing him on again. It makes the decision to show off with a buck much less glamorous for the horse if he then has to circle around for a while.

Make no mistake – bucking can be very dangerous. Do explore all the avenues available to try to overcome the behaviour sooner rather than later before it develops into more of a problem and someone gets hurt. Don't feel you 'should' be able to handle it on your own, or you 'shouldn't' be nervous. Be honest with yourself about your own capabilities and get specialist help if you think it's necessary. You know it makes sense!

Bolting – breaking out of control or trying to run away

Bolting can be one of the most frightening of the Baddies, depending on where you're heading – T-junctions of main roads are particularly unpleasant. As always, prevention is better than cure, so let's look first of all at the causes of bolting.

- The flight response is part of a horse's natural instinct, especially when he is frightened in any way. A horse has to bolt just once or twice around humans for it to become a habit.
- The horse has a painful mouth. There may be problems with his teeth or he's sore from the bit.
- The horse has a painful back.
- The horse has been overfed and underexercised.
- The rider is insecure and unbalanced and tips about in the saddle.
- The rider is heavy-handed and the horse's mouth has become completely dead to the pressure of the bit.
- The saddle is uncomfortable and/or too large.
- The rider wears the brand-new bright yellow raincoat that made the other horse buck.
- The horse is frightened by wearing an exercise sheet.
- The horse has never been properly schooled and doesn't understand from the aids the rider is using that he's meant to stop.
- The rider's aids are the complete opposite of what the horse has been taught is the signal to stop (as in a racehorse).
- The rider waves at a driver to thank him and it frightens the horse because he's not used to the movement or he thinks he's going to be hit.
- The horse has been 'held in an outline' too long (possibly a dressage horse).
- The horse is encouraged to gallop in the same area on every ride.
- The horse has a sudden fright, e.g. he's not comfortable with

CASE STUDY

Using circles

A couple of years ago I was at a horse show when someone's show pony was giving them trouble and my sister volunteered me to help. It was the first outdoor show of the year and, especially after enforced confinements due to foot and mouth disease, it was perfectly understandable for a horse to get a little overexcited. I went to the quietest corner I could find and just kept the circles going and was very attentive. Every now and again the pony would squeal with the pure joy and excitement of being out again with all these other horses around! As he settled I let the circles become gradually bigger. If he so much as bobbed his bottom, I went back to a tight circle again. I wasn't taking any chances! It took just 15 minutes or so for him to settle right down and walk round the showground like a gentleman. It's well worth working with the circles if you are in any doubt at all, because it only takes a couple of little overfresh accidents for people and horses to lose confidence in each other and bigger problems to develop.

plastic bags, umbrellas, loud noises or other daily occurrences when riding.

- The horse has been whipped when ridden – usually for being frightened of something, e.g. stopping at a fence or scary object, spooking at a car. Now when the rider moves her hands the horse thinks she's getting ready to hit him and runs for it.

True bolter versus running away

People who have been around horses for a long time will always differentiate between a horse that is simply running away and a true bolter, which is far more dangerous. If you are in any doubt about exactly which type you are dealing with, you must call in an experienced horseperson for advice.

It's my opinion that if you have a horse that runs off in a completely blind panic with no warning or for no discernible reason – especially

Below: 'Racehorse: An animal that can take several thousand people for a ride at the same time.'

one that will run through fences and hedges and into cars – it's better for all concerned if he is retired as a companion horse. It's not fair or kind to sell him to some unsuspecting people to discover the behaviour for themselves.

Stop that child!

The dangers of bolting may help convince you of the wisdom of schooling your horse and making sure he understands the aids before you start taking him on more ambitious rides. Young children are often taken on rides before they have any real control and it's horribly frightening for them when the pony decides to bolt for home, as ponies occasionally do when there's no one in charge up there.

The sensible thing to do is to have the pony on a lead rein, from on foot or from another horse, until the child can take control. Depending on how strong the pony is (and you are) and what equipment is available, have the line attached to a Dually halter on the schooling ring (ideal) or the bit and noseband or halter together – you don't want to pull the bit through the pony's mouth. Remember, the longer the line, the more leverage you have. On the other hand, you don't want to have such a long line and so much leverage that the pony jack-knifes at a pace fast enough to catapult the child such a distance that it takes all afternoon to find her!

Don't be tempted to use a severe bit in the early stages because this is likely to cause more problems than it solves. You must go right back to the beginning to teach your horse leg, seat and rein aids. Some lads and jockeys ride with very short stirrups so their legs don't touch the horse's sides. He may never even have felt legs down his sides and can't be expected to know what leg movement means. If your horse doesn't understand your aids, it's back to the drawing board with lots of slow work and schooling to help him.

> **What to do with a bolter?**
>
> 'My horse bolted with me at the weekend. He saw something he didn't like and bolted. I pulled and pulled on the reins but he didn't take any notice. Eventually he started to slow up and then stopped, thank goodness. Luckily no one was injured.
> My friend says to sell him as she wouldn't keep a bolter for any reason. I think it was because he's quite green. We only started him a couple of months ago and he's only ridden on average once a week since then. Would you sell him?'

Managing a horse that bolts

First of all, check and deal with or rule out physical problems. Ensure the horse is responding beautifully to his basic exercises on the ground.

Stop now!

Please be aware that every time the horse runs away, it encourages him to run away more. When I was 17 years old I had a formerly ill-treated showjumper that was improving well although he was still very strong to ride. I went for a lesson with a new trainer after I'd had him a year and she wanted to try out a theory she had that if you 'just let them gallop a bit, they'll tire and they won't pull again'. So I let him gallop and gallop and gallop around the indoor school. He loved it! It took me over six months to get him to settle again and not just want to gallop off all the time.

I suppose I was luckier than a friend of mine who was given similar advice. This was the time when you were told to smash eggs over horses' heads for rearing and whip them for bucking. My friend took the advice to gallop her horse over a ploughed field as 'that would slow him down'. Yes, it did but it also bust his tendon and he had to have a year's box rest.

Work on desensitizing him to various scary objects and go on to school him on long lines. Keep working on lightness by asking him for, say, a halt extremely gently with the reins and giving him a chance to respond before asking again. Remember your preparatory commands. Start to test him out by taking him to safe but slightly more out-in-the-open places. If he goes to bolt on the long lines, remember your one-rein stop. Don't even think of riding him in suspect areas until he's perfect on the long lines.

When it comes to reschooling from the saddle, again work on lightness. Remember that, if you can't ride properly, you are part of the problem and not of the solution. Go back to Chapter 4 and work through all the exercises until you can perform them with flying colours. Otherwise, you're not only wasting your time but you're going to get yourself and your horse injured.

Horses need to be taught how to stop properly. Often it's just assumed they know, or 'should' know. Give your horse several lessons in stopping and you'll see why you needed to go through 'Feel and Timing' and 'Please Ride Properly' first. You cannot teach your horse what you don't know yourself.

I much prefer an indoor school for reschooling. An enclosed manège is the next best thing, even a round pen, as you keep testing the waters.

Use the wall of the indoor school

Ride towards the wall and use your seat aids and the lightest of rein aids. The horse is going to have to stop at the wall anyway – you have just got to keep him straight. Gradually, he'll start to connect the aids with stopping (a conditioned response, i.e. he's had to learn it). Start at a walk and build up to a trot and then a canter as his responses become more reliable.

Transitions, transitions, transitions!

Ride your horse in interesting patterns, still in an enclosed area. The minute you feel the slightest unasked-for increase in pace, ask for a downward transition, from a canter down to a trot, from a trot down to a walk. It can work well to ride without contact. That doesn't mean having washing-line reins – just an inch of slack is 'without contact'. Then you can practise being really relaxed with him but still be in a position to put a little pressure on his mouth if you feel him picking up speed at all.

Bits and pieces

A stronger bit can sometimes be the answer to pulling up a horse, just as a martingale can help with a horse that throws his head too high. There is a proviso, however. You must understand that the effect may be temporary and it's absolutely necessary to reschool your horse at the same time. Otherwise, after a while the strong bit won't work for you

---

Mad? It's not me – it's everybody else!

Brain tumours are rare, as are other causes of 'madness' such as rabies (common in countries where I work though!), meningitis, encephalitis and liver failure. Most of these tend to cause depression, head-pressing or circling rather than manic behaviour, so I'd say that acute pain from any source or learned behaviour are much more likely to cause bolting. The only way to diagnose a brain tumour for certain is with a CT/MRI scan or post-mortem examination of the brain. The former is very expensive and not offered in many places. The latter is interesting but many owners don't like the thought of their horse having his head removed and opened after death, so few cases are reported.

Joy Pritchard, veterinary advisor for
Brooke Hospital for Animals

either and you'll be in that vicious circle of starting to use more and more severe bits with increasingly less effect, as the horse's mouth will get either very painful or appears to go totally dead.

A note for competition horses and ponies
Some showjumpers and eventers will start to be strong because they are excited by going fast in competition. In fact, the riders want them to pull a bit because you certainly don't want a horse backing off when you're coming up to a big fence. To avoid the trap of having to use a stronger and stronger bit in competition, if you find one that your horse goes well in at a show, save it for then and don't use it at home. Generally, you might go for a gentler bit at home and a stronger one at the show, but with some horses you'd do the complete opposite. Unfortunately, there are few easy answers with horses and bitting is yet another example of this. It's good that nowadays some companies hire out bits so you can find out what suits your horse without having to spend a fortune.

A few words about racehorses

When riding a former racehorse, go out with a sensible companion on a sensible companion horse, keep to a walk and trot and avoid open grass and canter tracks until much later. Introduce work such as circling or any collection slowly and carefully and, initially, in short sessions of a few minutes. Some racehorses will never have been out on their own or asked to lead 'the string' (particularly mares) so gradually build up the horse's confidence in being more independent. Long-reining lessons can pay dividends.

Remember, racehorses are taught to go faster when you tighten the reins, so the more you move your hands to tighten your grip, the faster you are signalling your horse to go. Racehorses have been taught to lean into the pressure of the jockey's hands when they run. They are never asked to stop promptly from a canter – it could damage the horse's legs, apart from sending the jockey standing in his stirrups straight over the horse's head. Racehorses just steady up gradually with their weight concentrated to the front of the body (none of this 'hocks underneath') until they're at a slower canter, then a trot, then a walk. They need to be completely reschooled for their new careers.

Disengaging the hindquarters – only use with caution (if at all)
Some Western riders in parts of the US and Australia use this exercise when riding by bringing one hand to the middle of the chest, causing a rein movement that, in effect, uncouples the horse's neck from the rest of his body and takes his hindquarters out of action. This is the same as the one-rein emergency stop used for long lining. Some riders teach their horse this at a walk and if the horse goes along so much as a little too fast, they immediately 'jack-knife' him in this way.

All horses should learn to yield to pressure throughout their bodies. Certainly, you should teach your horse to yield his head in each direction when he is ridden. He shouldn't hold any tension there because it will give your horse the opportunity to set his neck against you at a later time.

Above: Disengaging the hindquarters.

This method of stopping a horse from gathering speed can be very effective and it's one of the easiest to apply. However, depending on how fast the horse is going and how much force is used, it can cause considerable strain on the muscles at the base of the horse's neck and on the connective tissues of the neck bones in the area of the first rib. It's a worthwhile method to learn if horse and rider are going to be safer through using it, but the ultimate aim is for the horse and rider to gain greater trust in each other through better schooling.

When your schooling is perfect and you are ready to go out again

• Plan the route. Think carefully about the ride you are going on. On which part of the ride might your horse get too strong? Is it going to be safe to canter in circles until he gets tired or might you be heading towards a main road?

• Have someone on a reliable horse lead you. Children on ponies often have someone leading them so they can be pulled back in the case of an emergency. This is an excellent idea and it can work for adults as well. One thing to consider, though, is that it would be very dangerous to let the bolter go with the line attached and flying after him. Either be 100 per cent sure you're going to hold on to the line or double the line up so you have a quick release system if you were to let go. You don't want a horse running away with a line still attached to his head. It would be likely to frighten him even more.

• Anticipate what might happen. The instant you feel your horse picking up speed, ask him to halt immediately. Possibly circle him until he settles down. Disengage his hindquarters if that's the method you've decided to use.

• Be aware that pulling evenly on both reins only empowers your horse.

What to do if your horse bolts

If you realize you are being run away with and are out of control, it's essential to keep calm. Stand up a little in your stirrups (not leaning

Preventing jig-jogging

A horse that keeps breaking into a trot when he is meant to be walking is said to be jig-jogging. What you do not want to do is collect him up and hold with both hands. This is a way to activate the hindquarters and make him more powerful. It's far more effective to damp down the energy in his hind legs by gently taking up one rein and then the other until he realizes it's just easier to walk. Also take note of the advice in Chapter 7 about varying routes and getting off at different places. Lead him the last half-mile home (and just think how it will improve your thighs!).

forward necessarily) to avoid bouncing on the back of the saddle, which will only make the horse go faster – as will yelling or grabbing wildly with your hands (this is also frowned upon at parties).

One tactic is to anchor one hand, possibly by holding on to the mane, and pull the other one sharply upwards. If that doesn't work, you could try holding both reins in your two hands and pulling strongly and evenly to one side or the other to get his head to turn. If you are alongside a hedge or fence, turn the horse's neck into the fence while maintaining pressure with your outside leg to keep his body going straight. You'll sometimes see jockeys who are riding very strong horses position the horse's head over the rails on the way to the start of the race.

Look where you're heading and work out the safest route to take. If there isn't a safe route, e.g. you're heading for a main road, you need to think about getting your feet well out of the stirrups and bailing out at the softest spot. I hope you work through the other points thoroughly enough not to need this option.

Rearing

There are several reasons why a horse may rear when being ridden:

- He's in pain with a nerve pinching in his back.
- He's in pain with severe dental problems, such as a broken tooth.
- He's been overfed and underexercised.
- The saddle tree is pinching him at the front.
- The rider is heavy-handed and pulls on his mouth at the same time as gripping hard or kicking with her legs.
- He hasn't been properly schooled to the aids.
- A young horse may simply be fresh and excited (he may rear once in excitement and then never do it again).
- The rider tries a rein back but the horse is so stiff in his back and neck that he goes into a rear instead.
- The rider is nervous and anxious, making the horse nervous and anxious, too.

- He has been held in an outline for too long and rearing is a way for him to free himself from so much pressure.
- The bit is too severe. The longer the shank on a curb bit, the more likely the horse is to rear. Gag bits and any equipment that causes strong poll pressure are more likely to make a horse rear.
- He is very keen to go forward – when a group of other horses have gone in front, for example – and the rider restricts him.
- A sudden fright occurs in front of the horse.

- He is pointed towards an obstacle that he is unsure about, so he stops. He is made to face it and is hit with a whip. He feels his only choice it to go up.
- In the same way, if a horse is napping or jibbing and doesn't want to go forward and the rider whips him or uses a lot more leg pressure, this sends the horse up.
- A stallion or colt may think it makes him look really cool to the girls when he rears.
- A stallion or colt has a mare in front of him and he's in the mood for love.
- A stallion or colt has a gelding in front of him and he's got the idea that he should jump on anything presented before him.

Just a few years back, none of these reasons would have been considered. I'd be typing on my manual typewriter (can you imagine?) that you need to take half a dozen eggs with you on your next ride to crack over your horse's head when he next went to rear (again, can you imagine?). What's worrying is that there are still people out there giving the same sort of advice. One lady told me recently that where some people have been going wrong is that when they've cracked a bottle over the horse's head it's contained water but you actually need real blood to get him to think you've split his skull open – seriously, I was told this! I'd just like to say that I was around for some of those 'good old days' and I never heard of one horse being cured with a method like this – unless you consider killing and curing to be the same thing.

Above: 'Why is it that a woman will ignore homicidal tendencies in a horse, but will be furious at a man for leaving a toilet seat up?'

Anon

Left: 'Keep one leg on one side, the other leg on the other side, and your mind in the middle.'

Henry Taylor

What to do with a horse that rears

First of all, go through the list above to see if any of those reasons could apply to you or your horse. If you are not experienced with stallions and colts, get advice from a good stud hand as soon as possible. Stallions and colts can be beautifully mannered but they are not playthings. All your handling of them must be professional and businesslike. You don't need to be rough but you do need to move assertively around

Above: 'If you can't be a
Good Example then you'll
just have to be a Horrible
Warning.'

Catherine Aird

them, making sure they move away for you and not the other way around.
If they respect your personal space when you're on the ground, it solves
the majority of the problems. Do not wear perfume around them as the
pheromones can excite them. They need plenty of work to keep their
minds on the business in hand. (This may be the reason why teachers
encourage excessive amounts of sports at some boys' schools; it helps
keep the lads out of trouble.)

Watch someone else on your horse to see whether another rider has
the same problem and can give a reason for the behaviour.

I suggest you fit a neck strap so you have something to hold on to
in times of need and to prevent you making the problem worse and
even unbalancing the horse and pulling him over backwards. Some
horses that rear will give you a warning. They'll become very agitated,

snatch forward at the reins and give little bucks. You'll feel them rock backwards and forwards as they prepare to rear. Others will just go straight up in the air.

When working with a rearer, a safe, enclosed area with a soft surface is best (pretty obvious really). After the physical checks, including the equine dental technician and checking the saddle for comfort, ride the horse without a bit at all (you could try a Dually halter) in your safe arena to see if the problem is purely related to pressure on the mouth. This often is the case and although changing to a milder bit is a good move, sometimes the horse's fear of pain is so great that he's still going to rear at the slightest mouth pressure.

Are you part of the problem or part of the solution?

If you are riding a horse that might rear:
- don't ride with your stirrups too long;
- leave his mouth alone;
- don't attempt to ride him directly forward but take each rein out to the side loosely and ask him to go from side to side until he goes forward willingly.

If riding in the Dually takes away all the horse's inclination to rear, that's great, at least you know the cause. It doesn't mean you can never ride in a bit again. It just means some slow, gentle retraining needs to take place for the horse to gain trust in the rider's hands again. Part of that retraining may mean experimenting with having a bit in the horse's mouth but having the reins attached to the Dually or a hackamore. This way the horse stops equating the signals to slow down or collect himself with any frightening pressure in his mouth. Only when the horse has gained confidence with this should he be ridden off the bit. Long lining can be a real help. You can see how the horse accepts some contact from the bit, including using a rein back, before risking riding him.

If your horse says no, you either asked the wrong question or asked the question wrong.

Many of the Intelligent Horsemanship practitioners start their young horses in this way, teaching the horse the aids from a Dually halter before going on to a bit. A horse's mouth should be treated like the delicate living tissue that it is.

The horse that is tight and hollow in his back is the most likely type to rear. So schooling your horse to accept your weight aids as well as the bit is essential. Use your weight and seat correctly with no stiffness in the body, particularly through the shoulders, elbows and hands. Whether starting out or reschooling, it should never be necessary to pull a horse roughly in the mouth.

Using a pacifier

A pacifier is a piece of equipment that is used for racehorses that run on all-weather racetracks. It protects their eyes from the sand that the horses in front kick back. I've had experience of how painful it is as it hits your face. Most of the jockeys wear two pairs of goggles and pull the top ones down during the race when they get too dirty to see through. The pacifier is a bit like a pair of giant sieves over the horse's eyes. By restricting the animal's sight to a small degree, wearing one can relax the horse, or at least make him more cautious about where he's going. I have been up the gallops on some hard-pulling racehorses and in very thick fog, which occurs from time to time on Lambourn Downs, they go far more steadily.

Most people are familiar with blinkers, which are usually worn by driving horses and nervous or reluctant racehorses, but an advantage of the pacifier over blinkers is that you have a choice of where to restrict the horse's vision. Horses don't naturally like to go where they can't see, so if you put tape at the top of the pacifier it can stop the horse from attempting to rear. Experiments with material fly shields that fit over the horse's eyes have had equally good results and are a lot less expensive – a pacifier is usually over £100. Obviously, having your horse ridden out looking like 'The Fly' is not what you want in the long term, but it can break the pattern of this dangerous behaviour. Gradually reduce the taped area little by little to test out whether the horse is ready to go without 'The Fly' outfit altogether. If you wanted something less obvious-looking you could try a sheepskin cover over his browband to see if blocking out some of the light from above has any beneficial effect.

Key points
- It's important to get to the root of bad behaviour – don't just look at the symptoms, look at the causes.
- Always have thorough checks done for physical pain first of all.
- Check the equipment being used to see if that could be causing the problem.
- Would you pass the 'Please Ride Properly' tests from Chapter 4? Answer honestly.
- Make sure the horse's care routine is appropriate, i.e. food and exercise are balanced. Turned out? Stabled? Kept with company or alone?

Better bitless?

I recently visited the owner of a five-year-old Irish sports horse that had several problems including head-tossing, standing at the mounting block and, most dangerously, rearing. The head-tossing had resulted in facial injuries to the rider, such was its seriousness, and rearing was occurring up to a dozen or so times in a single schooling session. The owner had tried some sensible solutions, particularly in moving to a milder bit, which had reduced the rears per session. However, the lady was losing confidence and not enjoying her riding. She had already had the horse checked for physical problems including teeth, back and saddle checks.

Within the first few minutes of riding I felt as though the mare was waiting for something bad to happen. She was not nappy but appeared frightened to go forward. I told the owner that I suspected she'd been ridden by a very heavy-handed rider, possibly in a severe bit. The owner told me that, from the research she'd done about the mare's past, this was almost certainly correct. Riding with an extremely light contact on the rein and then a loose rein, the horse would still not take the rein forward or even attempt to stretch her neck down. Looking at her neck, she had an overdeveloped underside but almost no topline, suggesting that this was the way she had always carried herself. The horse did not rear for me, but I was asking nothing of her apart from some forward movement into no contact. It was a humble start but I felt that it was the only way to demonstrate to the horse that riding was not going to be painful, and that rearing did not have to be her solution. I went a step further and removed the bit altogether, attaching reins to the training rings of the Dually halter in place of the bridle.

In the owner's words, 'That was scary, but there was an instant transformation. She lengthened out, relaxed, stopped throwing her head, and looked like a different horse!'

Going bitless allowed the horse to stretch her neck forwards and down, which will help to develop her topline and strengthen her back. Hopefully, the horse will no longer associate work with discomfort.

I suggested that the owner should carry on with the Dually and then explore other options such as an English hackamore, Dr Cooks or scrawbrig bit. The bit could eventually be reintroduced, at first without the reins attached and still working bitless, and finally attaching to the bit and reschooling with a gentle contact. The owner's aim was to compete at dressage and currently bitless riding is not an option under Dressage Society rules.

To quote the owner again, after only a couple of bitless riding sessions, 'She doesn't rear, doesn't toss her head and suddenly you can feel the movement and there's a LOT of it! I thought that she moved well before but now it's like being on the back of an 18hh warmblood!'

Recommended Associate Sarah Dent

- Does the horse need to be completely restarted?
- Spending extra time schooling and bonding is going to be worthwhile.
- Be prepared to adopt specific riding techniques to help you cope with whatever the problem is, so you can be as safe and effective as possible.
- Sometimes specialist equipment can be useful and/or a specialist trainer must be considered.
- Learning to anticipate your horse's behaviour in order to prevent it or react accordingly is essential.

Ten out of ten for gate opening – absolutely guaranteed!

One of the exercises in Trec competitions is gate opening and I'm proud to say that my darling boy (that's Pie) got ten out of ten for his gate opening both times he competed. Now, getting ten out of ten for gate opening may not, in the grand scheme of things, be on a par with preventing global warming or reducing the landfill excess. However, success in anything often has several knock-on effects and that's why I'm encouraging you to follow this through.

It brings a certain satisfaction and confidence and, as the saying goes, 'success breeds success'. There is even a theory that if you study one thing very deeply, it enables you to communicate with other students studying a subject in depth, regardless of their area of expertise. In other words, perfect your gate opening and who knows what will be opening up for you next!

Quietly confident that gate opening wasn't rocket science and supported by my good friend and colleague, Ian Vandenberghe, Pie and I embarked on our first dummy run. Enthusiasm being one of our foremost qualities, we attacked the opening of the gate and Ian timed us at taking just under ten minutes.

'Not bad for a first attempt,' I said to Ian. 'With practise we could probably get it down to four or five minutes.'

I rang Monty in the US to give him a progress report, which was only fair as I had already informed him that Pie was coming on tour so we could show off our advanced gate-opening skills. They have timed competitions in gate opening in the US so, before impressing him with the promise we were showing, I asked, 'What's the fastest time they open gates in America, then?'

'If one is master of one thing and understands one thing well, one has at the same time insights into and understanding of many things.'

Vincent Van Gogh

Opposite: There are no problem horses, just horses with people problems.

Right: Perfecting angles of approach – 'The secret of getting ahead is getting started. The secret of getting started is breaking your complex, overwhelming tasks into small, manageable tasks, and then starting on the first one.'

Mark Twain

'About two to three seconds,' he said. Right. 'How are you doing?'

'Hmm, well, we haven't really got going yet,' I replied.

In a situation like this it pays to watch the experts – that's the theory, at least. So Ian trained to be a judge to increase his knowledge of how Trec works and came back from the training day with a video of some 'Treccers' in action during the World Championship in France. That seemed a good place to start our education and see how it was done. The video had a somewhat bewildering beginning, a variety of riders with maps hanging around their necks negotiating a forest, each of them going in different directions and obviously all hopelessly lost. Then we came to the obstacles section. I was watching keenly for tips at this point as my former careers in racing and showjumping hadn't called for much versatility, 'onwards' and 'upwards' more or less summing up what was needed. Watching the video, I picked up that you lost points for letting go of the gate until you had closed it, but was dubious of the wisdom of the only competitor on the video who 'didn't let go of the gate'. He hung on to the gate so tightly as his horse continued, that he dragged it off its hinges and pulled it 200 yards after him.

Make a plan

Having realized that even the very best didn't find gate opening as easy as it should be, I understood that it was going to take some work on my part and I started by making a list. All that you need to do to open gates successfully is:

1 Approach the gate from the correct angle (the commonest thing people get wrong) and teach your horse to:
2 Stand still.
3 Move backwards and forwards willingly in case you need to get closer to the latch.
4 Move in response to your leg pressure, in case you need him to get a bit closer to the gate.
5 Stand still while you lean over.
6 Do a turn on the forehand in one direction to get through.
7 Move off your leg in the other direction to close the gate.
8 Success!

1 *Approach the gate from the correct angle*
You do not ride directly at the gate, as many people do, and try to stretch down your horse's neck to reach it. For a gate opening outwards/away from you, ride towards the hinges of the gate and then

---

Deep study

She felt that if one could truly study transitions, one would see that a transition is a transition. The knowledge of them could be applied anywhere. I had to ask her to explain more. 'If a person studies one thing very well, and takes it very deep, that person can communicate with other deep students regardless of their respective expert subjects. The process is universal. That is why I contend that the process is more important than the subject. The paradox is that one needs a subject as a kind of password to get into the club. On the other hand, if a person studies many areas, many things, all superficially, that person ends up with a superficial knowledge. He can communicate with all other superficials, but not with persons of deep knowledge. Superficial learning is too wide and flat for me, it is also limiting. In order to arrive at a deep knowledge, there will have to be at least some superficial study. So the deep student can, if he wishes, work in either world. The superficials can only work in one. One good deep student can often help another.'

From The Songs of Horses *by Paul Belasik,*
published by J.A. Allen

towards the latch of the gate so your horse is alongside/parallel with the gate. If the gate opens towards you, just reverse the process.

2 *Stand still*

Note how standing still comes up repeatedly. It's an important discipline in so many different ways. Your horse should stand still. However, there are a lot of things that should happen but actually don't, and if this is one of those cases, you really need to get it right before going any further. Think about why your horse doesn't stand still. Does he never stand still? Is he a confirmed box walker in the stable, for instance? Or is it just at certain times, such as when you're mounting or dismounting? Is it any time you would like him to halt when you're riding or just when you get alongside a gate?

If he's generally hyperactive, would he be better off with more exercise and turnout? Is he getting too much energy from his food? Do be aware that many of the so-called 'quiet mixes' contain enough cereals and sugars to excite susceptible horses in the same way that some children become hyperactive through the 'E' numbers in foods. Top endurance rider Jane Van Lepp has an excellent range of sugar- and cereal-free feeds and her own horses clearly do very well on them.

If the horse is just fidgety while you're riding, could he be uncomfortable in some way? Don't be shy about getting expert help. In fact, it's well worth getting a recommended back expert to check your horse at least once a year even if things seem to be going well. Why wait until there is a problem? Is there some movement you're making that could be making him uncomfortable? Is his saddle, including any pads or girths or other equipment, pinching or irritating in some way?

What are you saying? Could you be giving him false cues? This is such an easy misunderstanding between horse and rider. Let's say you just want him to stand beside the gate but in your enthusiasm your breathing gets a bit faster, or you hold your breath. You squeeze your legs tighter and gather up the reins, which he associates with being collected to go at a faster pace or backing up, and as he fidgets and backs a little, you use your legs to keep him in place. Pretty soon he's doing a good impression of a piaffe or swinging his quarters round trying to figure out exactly what it is you're asking of him.

If you are a type A personality, someone who is always rushing around, it may have rubbed off on your horse. Practise standing still at various points on any ride and in schooling sessions, certainly when you first get on. Take the opportunity to stand a while to chat to your neighbours, letting your horse know that life isn't just one rush, rush, rush. So, all being well and if you are in a nice relaxed frame of mind, your horse should be able to stand still in various situations. If this is not the case, re-examine the previous paragraphs and perhaps consider getting experienced help.

Something that is well worth trying is to make a conscious effort to have a training session with absolutely no emotion involved. Label nothing as 'good' and nothing as 'bad'. Just observe. As things happen, ask yourself, 'I wonder how I made that happen?'

3 *Move backwards and forwards willingly, in case you need to get closer to the latch*

This can be achieved with basic gentle training, one step at a time. Ask and reward by releasing immediately on the response. In these training sessions keep everything very slow and easy. Be aware of your own breathing. Concentrate on your technique rather than just getting through, particularly in the early stages. In Trec competitions, the gate opening is not timed separately anyway. You can get maximum points by just riding through without taking your hand of the latch/attachment. It's only for your own fun that you might want to see if you can turn this into an art form!

4 *Move in response to your leg pressure, in case you need him to get a bit closer to the gate*

This isn't just a useful move for gate opening but essential if you are taking a horse out in traffic. As that big lorry comes roaring towards you, it's comforting to know you can just slide the horse right to the edge of the road to keep as far away as possible.

Effectively, the horse is moving sideways and you can start teaching him how to do it from the ground. Hold the rope just a few inches from the halter, arm outstretched, and press the fingers or knuckles of your other hand in his side, about where your heel would be. The instant he moves a little to the side, you stop that pressure and give him a little break – maybe spend a whole minute just giving him a stroke. Ask again and the instant he moves across, stop the pressure. As in nearly all horsemanship, the essence is in the timing. If you delay too long, you're likely to get an irritated, frustrated horse. If your timing is not

> **Talking to neighbours**
>
> My relationship with my neighbours has never really recovered since she called me over one evening as I was riding past on Pie and said, 'Do you know of another horse like that because my mother's looking for one?' I asked, 'What do you mean – a coloured horse?' And she said, 'Oh no, I just mean something old and quiet that someone might want to give away.' Pie was six at the time!

bad, you may achieve some results although your horse may be sluggish. If your timing is excellent, if you can remove the pressure as he thinks of moving over, you can get a really responsive, willing horse.

To prevent your horse from thinking he should move forward, you could try this with his head facing a wall or fence. If you think your horse is either chronically lazy or really finding it difficult to understand, find a twig with a few leaves attached and see if a tickling action will move him over. Sometimes you have to summon up energy yourself, maybe even give a little jump, to move him. Again, the most important part of this is the release/rest you give him when he gets it the slightest bit right. This is how he will understand what you want.

Once he has understood on the ground, you can progress to trying it from the saddle. Be aware this is not a natural movement for a horse and requires a lot of concentration on his part, so don't overdo it. Two or three steps at a time are more than enough to start with.

The movement is far more familiar in Western riding than English. One of the various ways you may be told to achieve it is to use a direct rein, i.e. bring your hand out in the direction you are going while putting more pressure on the outside stirrup. There is just one problem with this if you are leaning over to open a gate – can you guess what it is? That's right, you're very likely to be giving the horse the exact opposite directions to those you want! You lean over to open the gate with your right hand and put pressure in the right stirrup which the horse now associates with moving to the left. This is another common problem!

Below, left to right: The various stages of gate opening – 'I find that the harder I work, the more luck I seem to have.'
Thomas Jefferson

PERFECT PARTNERS

For this reason I suggest that when you start to teach side passes for gate opening, you concentrate mainly on little nudges with the outside leg to move him over. Just keep your weight fairly even in the stirrups and although you may open your hand in the direction in which you are going, try to keep this fairly subtle. Your main aim with the reins is gently to discourage the horse from going forward so as not to encourage confusion later on.

Summary

Start with two or three steps sideways with your horse's head facing a fence/wall and build up to five or six steps. Progress to sideways steps in the open, perhaps over a pole. Next, ride alongside a gate but be one or two strides out so you have to ask your horse to step sideways. Relax and give him lots of praise once he's pressed against the gate.

Get it clear in your own mind: you want him to feel that being pressed against that gate is a great place to be. How will you do that?

5 *Standing still while you lean over*

Standing still while you're sitting upright is now easy, but standing still as you lean over slightly is a key time for those accidental cues. Ask someone to watch your legs and hands, and your horse's expression, to see if they can spot any inadvertent messages you may be sending to your horse. He may just need desensitizing to the leaning over, i.e. to be taught that leaning over does not mean 'move' until further aids are given. Practice is in order.

Ask him to stand still, lean over a little and try to catch him doing something right. If he continues to stand for a few seconds, sit back up and praise him with rubs on his neck, if that's what he likes, and then lean over again. If he moves off, just gently move him back to the halt position and encourage him to relax before leaning over again. This takes as long as it takes. If your horse finds it particularly difficult to grasp, you may want to divide the training into mini sessions at the end of each ride so that when he gets it right and relaxes, you can reward him by getting off and finishing his work for the day.

Ironically, once you get the gate opening really nifty, you may not need your horse to stand still because the exercise will be a continuous movement. However, the ability to stand and relax at appropriate moments is very helpful when you start to work on gate opening and invaluable in other areas.

An amateur will practise until they can get it right. A professional will practise until they can't get it wrong.

6 *Do a turn on the forehand in one direction to get through*
The definition of a turn on the forehand is 'the horse yields away from the rider's leg when he's at a standstill. His front legs remain more or less on the same spot while the hindquarters make a 180-degree turn around the forehand, so that the horse ends up facing the opposite direction.'

You are now standing alongside the gate, which is on your right-hand side. Holding both reins in your left hand, you have to unclip the gate, keeping hold of whichever part is appropriate (and is going to remain easiest to keep hold of). You now need your horse to press against the gate to push it open wide enough for you to walk through. As the gate is opening, you are going to do a turn on the forehand to the left to get him in position to walk through. In this case, the turn will be a 90-degree pivot and not a full turn.

How to do a turn on the forehand to the left
Sit evenly and move your right leg behind the girth for the sideways movement. Have the left leg on the girth for support and to stop him moving sideways too quickly. Just vibrate the right hand to flex him at the poll. Keep the left hand steady and supporting so his neck remains fairly straight. I'd advise you to practise with two hands to start with but eventually you're going to have to do this one-handed. Then you'll have the right rein slightly shorter and 'tweak' or vibrate with the outside fingers. Ideally, the horse will step over and in front of the left hind leg with his outside right.

It's a good idea to practise the 180-degree turn alongside a fence and then, when that is getting too easy, go on to the gate. The turn on the forehand is not an exercise you want to practise excessively. Being on the forehand is usually something to avoid and this exercise is putting the centre of balance on the forehand – hence its name. As with all the exercises, make sure your horse is getting lots of wins and let him know when he's getting it right. We all work better for a few strokes.

7 *Move off your leg in the other direction to close the gate*
Ride through the gate holding the latch and as soon as your horse is completely through, use your left leg to move him over with sideways steps, in the other direction. Get in close enough to latch the gate.

'Show me a horse who's been trained and trained and trained and still does not obey, and I'll tell you who the slow learner is!'

8 *Success!*
Now the most important advice of all – before you ride off, don't forget to let go of the gate!

Don't immediately rush off. Sigh and stroke your horse for a while. Explain to him that now the two of you have perfected gate opening, who knows what you might accomplish next.

Even if you never see another gate, once you've gone through these exercises successfully it means you will have a horse that will stand calmly, step forwards, step backwards, step sideways and do a turn on the forehand, all with just the gentlest requests. Fantastic!

Key points

- Have a 'party piece', i.e. get very good at one thing. What's it going to be? Start practising now!
- Think through your approach carefully.
- Break tricky tasks into bite-sized pieces.
- Ask a friend to read the instructions in this chapter out to you while you're on your horse so you can concentrate on the aids you're giving your horse.
- Practise these steps separately before putting them all together.
- Always be aware of what signals you are giving your horse. How should he know which ones he should take notice of and which ones to ignore?

Putting the Intelligence into Horsemanship

10

Ignorance

'Only ignorance! Only ignorance! How can you talk about only ignorance? Don't you know that it is the worst thing in the world, next to wickedness? And which does the most mischief heaven only knows. If people can say "Oh! I did not know, I did not mean any harm" they think it is all right.'

From Black Beauty *by Anna Sewell*

What qualities would you choose for your other half in a relationship if that other half was going to be responsible for all your needs? Crucial decisions such as when you had to say goodbye to your mother, never to see her again, what you ate, where you stayed, your exercise programme, what you wore and who were to be your friends would all be made for you. Would you be looking for someone you could trust and respect who was sensitive and reliable? Who was educated? 'Educated'? Is that a fair request? It's not as if your horse advertised for you in the personal column of *The Times*, after all!

In fact, education is something you owe your horse. In these times of easy access to information there is just as much suffering caused by ignorance as there ever was. I'm not just talking about Egypt and India where such crazy practices as ear cutting and eye glassing* are commonplace. In many western

Quack cures

* Ear cutting is the practice of slitting a donkey's ears lengthwise and is used for a variety of ailments. Some owners think it can ease colic, others that it confers resistance to tetanus. All it does is cause pain. In some regions a working equine animal that develops a cloudy eye is treated by eye glassing – where ground glass is blown into the eye in the belief that this will clear the vision. Instead, the animal suffers and usually becomes blind.

Information from the
Brooke Hospital for Animals, 2004

countries, horses are suffering often from misplaced kindness. Some are overfed and in agony from laminitis, others are overprotected and develop neurotic habits similar to psychotic people. Unable to settle for a moment, they walk round and round in circles or weave to and fro. Some poor confused horses are being trained to perform undesirable behaviours by well-meaning owners (see Chapter 2) and are then punished for them.

How should mistreatment be defined?

Mistreatment is often associated with evil but is far more likely to be caused by ignorance or insensitivity. Take the following story, for example. At a horse show one day a young man I knew, who worked with horses, called over to me, 'Hi Kelly. How are you doing? You know, I've got a horse I could do with you looking at.' I'd given him advice previously about a racehorse that wouldn't go into the starting stalls. 'Mind you,' he added with a chuckle, 'I've done something you wouldn't quite approve of.'

Now, I've been in the horse world long enough to know what goes on. I haven't just been drifting around with the fairies. So I said, 'You've been giving him electric shocks, haven't you?'

'I've just buzzed him a few times,' he said.

'Don't tell me,' I said, 'and now he's kicking out at you?'

'Well, it's not that so much, but the b****** has just gone lairy on me. Do you know, he won't go near the stalls at all now. So...' (and this is the punchline) '... I was thinking of sending him to Joe Bloggs [name changed to protect the guilty!] up the road, but you know,' he paused with a regretful shake of his head, 'I don't want to do that. He's just so awful hard on them.'

> **A very worthwhile question**
>
> What's the difference between intelligent people and stupid people? Well, intelligent people do intelligent things and stupid people do stupid things. Just try asking yourself this question from time to time: 'Is this an intelligent thing to do or a stupid thing to do?' It could save you a great deal of aggravation – it may even save your life.

So there we have it. This guy was giving the horse electric shocks but was too soft to send the horse on. What an earth was the other man going to do to the poor horse that was worse?

I am so pleased that the young man told me about the horse. Being judgemental about people doesn't help. As Maya Angelou said, 'I was doing the best I knew how to at the time. If I'd have known better I'd have done better.' I was able to get someone to help him so he could achieve the results he wanted and at the same time have a calmer and more confident horse. Maybe we can all start making up for our past mistakes when we were 'doing the best we knew' by trying to use some intelligent horsemanship and think from the horse's point of view.

So what is intelligent horsemanship?

At first, this was a working title for the courses we were planning, but as so often happens, the name stuck. After all, that is what we are trying to achieve – an intelligent approach to working with horses that applies to all disciplines and all riders. So whether you want to lead your horse safely out to the field each day and enjoy hacking out more than you do, or to win top-class races, show classes or showjumping competitions, this approach is appropriate.

What does 'intelligent' mean? From the Oxford Dictionary we have 'having the faculty of understanding', 'having or showing a high degree of understanding' and being 'an intelligent or rational being'. It doesn't say anything about 'being against traditional methods' or, indeed, being against anything. It doesn't say 'a system of working'. While we can try to put together as many helpful guidelines as possible, we're still going to have to be prepared to adjust and adapt to each individual situation – isn't that a positive rather than a negative? It's precisely this constant need for flexibility and re-assessment that makes the work so intriguing and satisfying.

We should be thinking and questioning all the time and not simply doing something because everyone else does, or because it has always been done that way. Educate yourself to think, read, research and ask questions even of the people you do not agree with. They may have a point or a valid reason for doing something and although you might decide, 'Well, I'll never do that with my horse,' that's learning, too.

> 'Two things are infinite: the universe and the stupidity of mankind. And I'm not yet quite certain about the universe.'
>
> **Albert Einstein**

Common sense plus

It's popular to believe that everything can be solved by 'good old common sense', but if you are not experienced in a subject and simply don't know the most likely thing to happen, common sense isn't much help. For instance, apply common sense to these questions:

- How long was the 100 years war?
- Where do Chinese gooseberries come from?
- If an older horseperson asks you to give a horse chilled water, what temperature should it be?

The answers are:

- The 100 years war lasted 116 years.
- Chinese gooseberries come from New Zealand.
- Chilled water means water with the chill taken off, i.e. lukewarm.

I've already mentioned how certain things can be counter-intuitive, i.e. the right thing to do is the exact opposite of what you'd expect. Only experience, or the benefit of other people's experience, will teach us what to look out for, so keep studying your subject.

Intense emotional reactions can sometimes overwhelm the rational brain, forcing us to over-react or misunderstand the situation. Daniel Golman called this 'emotional intelligence'. It's even easier to fall victim to this when you are tired, unhappy or under stress. Lack of time in any situation rarely brings out the best in us. How you respond to a question as you're rushing out the door is often different from how you'd respond if you were asked the same question as you sip a long cool drink in a restaurant.

Give yourself the best chance to be a partner your horse can trust and respect. If ever you feel you can't handle a situation with your horse, if you're starting to lose patience, or lose faith in yourself or your horse, look at the list and make sure you have more ticks on the 'Friends' side than on the 'Enemies'. Keep giving yourself the best chance to succeed.

Enemies of intelligence

Lack of experience in the subject
Stress and tiredness
Lack of time and having to hurry a job
Getting over emotional upheavals
Overconfidence bordering on arrogance
Complacency – not bothering to think things through
Laziness

Friends of intelligence

Experience in the subject
Having the time to think
Dedication
Sense of responsibility
Understanding that there is always more to learn
Flexibility
Knowing what you are capable of at any given time
An ability and willingness to think things through – 'what's the likely outcome of this?'

There's a difference between being open-minded and giving your brains away

Please remember that there is no substitute for effective techniques, knowledge, experience and practising your skills consistently. The promise is only that if you use your awareness in tandem with all these, it will enhance your work with your horse immeasurably. Awareness of feelings and even tuning into a 'higher plane' is wonderful, but it's best to stay grounded in the real 21st century world at the same time. Some well-meaning person may tell you that animals are so much cleverer than people because they have this amazing sixth sense, so how come my cat, who was quite brilliant in every way, ran in front of a car and got run over? In the modern world our animals rely on a great deal of protection from us and will often meet a hasty end if we're not extremely attentive to their practical welfare. Animal healer Margrit Coates once told me that some people really cause her concern when she goes to visit their horses. They might have crystals hanging in one corner, have flower remedies in the water and have feng shuied the tack room after dowsing everyone for negative vibes. Margrit, who is very grounded in reality in spite of her gifts, will have to tell them,

'Look, before we go any further I think it's important you know that this horse needs a good meal.' Or she might have to say, 'I'm sorry but your horse needs a vet immediately.'

Don't be fooled into believing that there is one great answer out there and you can abdicate responsibility. Ultimately you're the one responsible for your horse and for your lives together. I have known people to be so seduced by a particular method that they have ended up being responsible for the death of their horse. One example was when a horse died of laminitis after invasive feet trimming. The owner's only experience of the subject was a weekend course. Another owner I knew of refused to put a rug on a horse when he was suffering from the cold because he must be kept 'naturally' (but Arabs wouldn't 'naturally' live in Yorkshire!). One lady owner would not bring her very sick horse into a shelter because she believed it would be morally wrong to put 'pressure' on the horse by leading him in a headcollar. These were not deliberately wicked people. It was almost as if in their quest to be open-minded they had developed complete tunnel vision.

Below: Not *everyone* is convinced about keeping horses 'naturally'!

Please, never give your inner sense and compassion away to 'a method'. Remember to keep that journal for you and your horse. Does he seem comfortable? Does he seem relaxed? Does anything change in his character as other factors change around him? Read through your discoveries from time to time. You may find all the answers you need in there!

See into the future with intelligent horsemanship

Here's a story of how a horse came to us because he 'became a problem horse'. We'll call him Blackie. The owners were nice people and had owned him from early on in his life. They brought him up well and by the time he was three years old he was already well handled and had been gently introduced to his first saddle without stress of any kind. He was so good they were even long lining him gently around their property. As they hadn't started a young horse before, though, and he was very important to them, they thought it was the right thing to do to send him to a professional to be introduced to a rider and for further schooling.

The professional who took over decided to get on Blackie for the first time without using a saddle or bridle. Blackie was scared and moved away sharply and the professional promptly fell off. The professional then said that what Blackie needed was 'desensitizing' and so he tied plastic bags to his tail and let him loose in a large field. This was terrifying to Blackie and, as he had the freedom to run, that's what he did – as far and as fast as he could, including through several fences. It took months of patient work for Blackie to overcome his fear of plastic bags, humans and virtually anything else that moved. It was a great shame for the owners and I have no idea of what the professional could have been thinking. He couldn't have been very experienced with horses or he would have known that one of the most damaging things that can happen to a horse is for him to get loose in a large open space while perceiving something is 'chasing him'.

A small but determined number of the Intelligent Horsemanship students want to go on to work with horses themselves. Those that are successful soon realize they need to study human psychology as much as they need to learn about horses because people do extraordinary things, sometimes after their horse returns home from training. There was one instance of a horse that had been a severe bucker. He had been in training for a couple of months to overcome this dangerous

'Believe those who are seeking the truth. Doubt those who find it.'

André Gide

I was impressed by a story I heard from one of my students, a teacher herself. A little while ago a woman came to her for a riding lesson and before she had even got on, the horse did something unasked for and the woman struck him really hard three times with a dressage whip. The teacher (our heroine) took a deep breath and carried on with the lesson. Afterwards, people at the yard were pretty judgemental. A common reaction was, 'I don't know how you could continue giving the lesson after that awful women did that.' The teacher answered, 'Because she needed my help more than anyone I've ever taught.' Later during that lesson, the whip lady was in tears. She felt bad about what she'd done but really it was just symbolic of her life in general. She talked to the teacher about the stresses she was under and later chose to go to anger management classes.

---

habit. The rider rode him before she took him home and she was happy that he was now behaving beautifully. She was told that he must not be allowed to forget his training and was advised to ride him every day for some time until he was completely trustworthy. Unfortunately, when she took him home she turned him out for several months while she was busy with other things. Then one day she was out in the field and thought how lovely it would be to get on him with no saddle or bridle. You don't need more than one guess as to what happened do you?

I'm hoping that by telling these stories you'll start to predict what's going to happen. That's what you gain with experience. It's almost like gaining the ability to see into the future. Let's see if you can predict this one. Some people buy a young horse and decide to start him themselves. They take him into a big field to lunge him. 'He was going quite nicely so we decided to put his first saddle on,'just loosely', to see how he'd be.' Have you guessed yet? That's right, he became severely traumatized after getting loose in the field when the saddle slipped underneath him and around his stifle area. Here's another, from a letter I received: 'My young horse was being really kind in the stable and was happy wearing his first saddle. However, I said to my friend at the time 'I think this is a mistake getting on him for the first time in the big field, especially as all his friends are out there...'

> 'If at first you don't succeed – find someone who knows what they're doing.'

Choose your trainer carefully

Before you send your horse away to a trainer, I would strongly advise you to ask for three personal references about similar work they have done. Visit or ask a friend to visit the yard, and visit the horse within the first few days to see how he's settling in. I cannot count the number of 'problem' horses I have worked with at demonstrations when the owner has said, 'He seemed fine and then we sent him away to a professional trainer and...'

Please understand that I'm not criticizing all professional trainers. I'm just suggesting that some people out there are not as professional as they should be. If you are a horse owner, you have to make it your responsibility to send your horse to the best place possible. Read *Tom Brown's Schooldays* if you need any convincing how bad things can get if a parent or caring person doesn't ask careful questions to find out exactly what's going on. Personally, I would be very suspicious of a trainer who discouraged me from visiting my horse. I have heard of trainers forbidding the owner to visit on the excuse that 'it might unsettle the horse'. Even more remarkably, the owners have accepted this!

> **Story from a Swedish demonstration**
>
> 'I sent him away to a professional trainer to be broken in. He was there for two years. When I went to pick him up they said there was no one there to show me him being ridden but I could ride him myself if I wanted to try. I paid the final money owing and they said they wouldn't be responsible for anything that happened to me. When I got him home and tried to ride him he bolted straight away.'

One of the reasons the system of Intelligent Horsemanship Recommended Associates was set up was to provide a service that owners could trust. Nobody (and no organisation) is infallible but all the Recommended Associates are regularly evaluated and are accountable to the Association should anyone not be completely satisfied with the work that has been done with their horse.

When you go to collect your horse, do make sure you fully understand what has been done with him and what the trainer feels is a sensible programme for you to follow in the future. Recommended Associates include written instructions to owners when the horses are collected because it's helpful for owners to have something to refer to when they get home. Assumptions cause more problems than anything else in communication. The trainer may assume you understand the stage the horse is at and what you should do, while you assume the horse is now completely quiet and you can do anything you like with him. Never assume!

The freedoms horses are entitled to enjoy

As I have done my best to explain, Intelligent Horsemanship is as much about understanding ourselves as about understanding horses. Understanding ourselves is often by far the most difficult and complicated part. As for understanding horses, it's a lifetime study but here are a few points to bear in mind.

Horses have their own particular needs so we should learn as much about horse welfare as possible. Following the model for farm animals, they are entitled to five basic freedoms:

1 freedom from thirst, hunger and malnutrition;
2 freedom from physical and thermal discomfort;
3 freedom from pain, injury and disease;
4 freedom to express most patterns of normal behaviour;
5 freedom from fear and distress.

If you look around, are you aware of any horses not receiving these five freedoms? Remember, malnutrition means overfeeding as well as underfeeding. Thermal discomfort? What about horses that have been clipped and are then expected to fend for themselves? I've seen a great many horses in pain due to badly fitting saddles and I've seen horses in fear and distress as part of their training. However, we are limited in what we can do for other people's horses and we must first look closely at the care of our own. We don't live in a perfect world but if we all keep making small changes in the right direction, maybe one day we will.

> The fact that horses adapt so well to different circumstances is the reason they are subject to so much abuse. Just because a horse is not complaining, it doesn't necessarily follow that he is happy and comfortable. In the wild an injured animal will be the most attractive to a predator, so horses have evolved to hide their pain as much as they can.

Listen to your horse

Pie is the all-time best loader into a horsebox. After my last demonstration on the November 2003 tour, as we arrived home from Cornwall at 4 a.m., I led Pie out of the horsebox, handed him to Ian Vandenberghe and then walked back into the horsebox to fetch something, and Pie started to follow me back in! On Monty's tour in February

2004, Pie came along again to show some of his party pieces. He travelled in the horsebox with Recommended Associate Dan Wilson looking after him when I wasn't around. They would come along a little later to each venue as some of the rest of us went ahead to start to get things ready.

When they arrived at Birchenly Manor, Dan told me that Pie had been a bit reluctant to load that morning. What do you think Dan did? You might think that he'd have put a Dually halter on him, backed him up, kept him moving his feet around. No, that's not what he did at all. He immediately thought, 'What could it be that's making him not want to load?' He decided it was the way other things were packed in the horsebox, which meant Pie had to travel right at the back. With some help, Dan re-jigged the contents around so that everything was further forward. He then went back and got a bowl of food. Pie thought that was fair compensation for the inconvenience he had suffered. Did you think none of us would ever do something like that? As you get to know your horse, you adapt your methods to the circumstances. Dan knows

Below: The art is to get your horse to *want* to load in the horsebox.

Pie well and is one of the people with whom I have perfect confidence in leaving him.

Make travelling comfortable for your horse

- Airborne dust is prevalent and unpleasant for horses when travelling. Hose out your horsebox or trailer regularly and have a dust-free floor surface. Either soak the hay or use haylage.
- If you are using a haynet, don't use one with tiny holes. Try to avoid these haynets at all times because in order to eat from them, horses have to twist their heads and necks unnaturally to pull the hay out. Find another way to slow your horse's hay consumption if that's necessary. Don't give your horse's physiotherapist more work than she can handle.

- Giant travel boots cause more problems than they help. I've used them myself in the past, thinking that they were helpful in protecting the horse. What I've found in practice is that horses think they are drowning in a swamp when wearing this enormous amount of padding around their legs. The boots are very apt to make a horse travel badly, especially if they start to slip down and the horse treads on them. If you want protection on your horse's legs learn how to put bandages on correctly or use closer fitting boots.

Since then, one of my students, Steve King, has done a project on this subject, and I've learned that it is far less comfortable for a horse to travel behind the rear axle of the horsebox because there is so much up and down movement. At the time, Monty told us about when he travelled around America in a very large coach. There was a bed right at the back but it was impossible to sleep in it because you'd get so 'seasick'. Not only was this a learning curve about the most comfortable place for a horse to travel, but when I got the horsebox home from that part of the tour I had it checked over mechanically and found that the shock absorbers had worn out at the back. As you can imagine, this gave me major feelings of guilt.

Where is your horse going to live?

Think very carefully before buying a horse and be sure you can provide the necessary facilities, finance and time available to give him a happy and comfortable life. Many horses can live outside very comfortably all year round, so long as they have good shelter, fresh water and a caring owner who checks daily that they are well and still in the field they are meant to be in – and one who understands that extra food, shelter, rugs or veterinary care may sometimes be necessary.

Some people have got the idea that natural horsemanship means leaving the horse out to fend for himself. To be honest, if we were really practising natural horsemanship, we wouldn't be touching horses at all.

Only the strongest horses survive and reproduce in the wild but many horses in Britain haven't been bred to tough things out, so leaving them to fend for themselves is not an option.

Another very important factor is that in truly natural conditions the horse would have a great deal of choice about where to go at any given time of the day or night and in all seasons. He could seek out the most comfortable places for himself. Please do not surround a horse with electric fencing on the top of a hill or down in a bog where he can't get out of the wet or wind and rain, and think this is 'natural' to a horse.

Many people aren't fortunate enough to have unlimited access for horses to be turned out, particularly in the winter. Also, many horses suffer more in the spring and summer through heat and the risk of laminitis than in the winter, and have to be stabled. This can put severe restrictions on the patterns of normal behaviour, listed in the five freedoms. Normal behaviour includes being around other horses, mutual grooming, moving freely, including rolling. Remember that horses eat off the ground naturally. It's better for their teeth, their backs and their nasal passages and can easily be arranged in a stable.

Most horses need at least 6 square metres (roughly 65 square feet) to roll right over as they would in a field and it's good to see that nowadays some successful racehorse trainers allow their horses free time in specially built, high paddocks. My father always had a sand ring where his racehorses could have a good roll after work. If horses have to stay inside all winter, a barn arrangement can be ideal where at least they can move around and touch each other. A horse's well-being and mental health are going to benefit greatly if he can at least have a few hours turned out each day, even in a barn.

Pair bonding

Lifelong pair bonds are very unlikely to happen in the wild or where a number of horses are kept outside together. A horse may choose to spend time with another of the same age and height but the pairing is quite likely to change. Also, a horse's influence changes from year to

Horse or duck?

I once received a video from someone who said her horse was agoraphobic (phobic about going outside). You saw the person turn her horse out of his comfortable stable directly into a small paddock that was covered with at least six inches of water. The horse splashed around for a while and then came back into his stable. I think this was less about the horse being agoraphobic than not being a duck!

year as the youngsters mature and the older ones step down somewhat. These changes are perfectly natural in the wild. Mares are occupied with their foals. Stallions oversee their mares. Bachelors are friends with other bachelors for as long as it's convenient, i.e. until a more attractive offer comes along (you get people like that as well).

Pair bonding is often man-made. It can sometimes happen when a limited number of horses are kept together. Sometimes people deliberately keep two horses together so they will bond before being turned out in a bigger herd.

While it's unfair to keep a horse on his own, having two can mean they bond too much and make an enormous fuss every time the other horse is out of sight. With Pie and Floyd, in order to avoid separation anxiety I also have a rescue pony, Herbie. We call him a 'companion' pony thinking it's good for his self esteem. Nowadays there's a great new career opening for these former rescue ponies. The three of them are turned out together during the day, and at night they can see each other although Herbie is stabled between the big boys.

Pie and Floyd are shod when they compete but have around three months off during the winter with no shoes, and are allowed more freedom. This is not a hard and fast rule but it works well for them. We have to do the best we can for each individual situation. Let's face it, it's unlikely that any of us is ever going to be perfect, but if we aim as high as we can, at least we'll have the satisfaction of knowing we've reached the highest standards of which we are capable. Do the horses in your life deserve any less?

Are you a perfect partner for your horse?

- On cold mornings, make sure the bit isn't freezing before you put it in his mouth.
- Be careful not to bang his teeth when putting in or removing the bit.
- Don't throw his rug on from the near side so the buckles hit his legs as it goes over his back.
- Make sure when tacking up not to smack his legs with the girth buckles.
- Do the girth up gently. Do not do it fully in one go.

CASE STUDY

More and more people are finding a 'better way'

A couple of years ago, I received a letter that said, 'I've read your articles and seen one of your demonstrations and I totally believe in what you do. However, the other day I had a horrible experience that I wondered if you could help me understand. There is a horse in my yard that doesn't load well. Having seen your demonstration, I thought I would train him in the same way and in a calm and fair manner. After just a short while, when I thought I was making progress, a man in charge of the yard came over and told the owner I was wasting time. He kicked the horse several times in the stomach and the horse went in the trailer. He regularly treats horses like this and can often get better results than me. It just doesn't seem right. I want to believe in your methods but why would this be?'

I found it a thought-provoking question. Sadly, I can't say punishment never works for horses. Fear and pain are a motivator for horses and humans. There are several things to consider, though. One is that people who work in this way have to watch their backs (perhaps literally). I have heard more than a few stories of people who were very hard on horses getting injured when that horse kicked out next time they got near it, or ducked out from jumping a fence and caught the

rider out. Just from a safety point of view, some of us don't want to have to live like that.

The second point to consider is more fundamental and revolves around how you want to live your life. If someone chooses to be a tyrant and a bully, it doesn't mean you have to be one too.

I replied along these lines and the lady was nice enough to write back to thank me. She said she'd changed yards and felt a lot better. That exchange wasn't at the forefront of my mind about a year later when I was running a five-day course. At the introductory meeting, students generally say a little about themselves, their experience and why they've come on the course (it's not compulsory). On this occasion, one gentleman explained, 'You wrote a letter to a friend of mine,' and repeated the above story. He said he was really impressed that I'd taken the time to reply in such detail. 'Well, that's nice,' I thought. It was the next bit that gave me an emotional jolt. He said, 'You see, I was the person who kicked the horse. That's how I've always been around horses. She was in tears as she gave me your letter to read to explain how she felt. She took her horses away that day and we haven't spoken since. It was then I decided it was time for me to look at a different way of doing things.'

- Make sure he's warm/cool enough.
- Do not use dirty boots, tack or numnahs because they will rub and be uncomfortable.
- Make sure to remove tack or loosen the girth whenever possible between classes at shows.
- Be careful not to squash his ears when putting on the bridle.
- Where possible, mount from a block instead of the ground.
- When mounting or dismounting, do not kick his back.
- Take the time to learn as much about horse nutrition, veterinary care, physiology and equine needs as you possibly can.
- Avoid grooming him or messing about with him when he's eating his feed.
- Do not drag the saddle off with the girth hanging. Place it over the saddle and then lift off gently.
- Always acknowledge your horse when entering his stable.
- Give him reasonable warning before you do anything with him.
- Make sure he is standing square and can balance properly before lifting a hoof.
- Place his feet down gently after you've picked them up.
- Make sure you allow plenty of clearance for your horse when going through gates or doorways.
- He will appreciate a gentle rub or stroke on the neck or wither more than a hard slap, however well intentioned.
- Make sure you place his (perfectly fitting) saddle gently on his back, and that you place your bottom gently in the saddle!
- Be sure that he is fit enough to do what you are asking him to do.
- Make sure he understands your requests.
- Listen to your horse. 'Bad' behaviour is often his only way of letting you know that something is wrong.
- Drive slowly and gently when driving lorries or towing trailers with horses inside.
- At shows, make sure he has shade while tethered next to the horsebox or lorry.
- Put his needs first, e.g. at shows, make sure he is fed and watered before you are.
- Don't be afraid to get specialist help when you need it.

'Shoot for the moon. Even if you miss, you will land among the stars.'

Les Brown

'My treasures do not clink together nor glitter. They gleam in the sun and neigh in the night.'

Gypsy saying

Index

Acknowledgments

I would like to thank all those of my students and the Intelligent Horsemanship Recommended Associates who gave me case studies and stories for this book, especially Ally Sixsmith and Charlie Davis for exchanging endless emails on long winter evenings reassuring me it would all make sense eventually. Also Dr Francis Burton for 'running his eye over' the more scientific parts of this book. I am very grateful to my friend and colleague Nicole Golding who helped enormously in putting this book together, and the Ebury team; particularly Carey Smith, Sarah Lavelle, Katherine Hockley, Roger Hammond and Roger Daniels for their painstaking work and enthusiasm.

Thanks are due to the Intelligent Horsemanship office team who worked above and beyond the call of duty. Gitte Monahan, who is pictured working at her computer on the Pilates ball, was a fantastic help with the photographs and general support, and Rosie Jones, who helps us, became so obsessed with working on the quotes that for some time everything she said was in inverted commas. Brenda Whelehan, Shaun Whelehan and Linda Dibbens deserve a special mention for never saying, even if they thought it, 'Is this book ever going to get finished?'

I really must thank my niece Daisy O'Halloran for making sure I stay aware of the 'real world' of horsemanship and also for bringing the wonderful Pie into my life. (Incidentally, I do apologise that there are really not enough photographs of him in this book.)

Intelligent Horsemanship would not have existed without the innovative ideas of my fabulous friend Angela Vince and would not have been nearly so much fun without those I see on a regular basis namely, Ian and Sandy Vandenberghe, Linda Ruffle, Sandra Williams, Grant Bazin and Dan Wilson.

And, finally, it is difficult to put into words how much I owe to Monty Roberts. All I know is I'm going to have to be working for a very long time if I'm ever to give back to people and horses all that he has given to me.

Useful addresses

For information on Intelligent Horsemanship courses, demonstrations, shopping, help with your horse or recommended reading see our website:
www.intelligenthorsemanship.co.uk

or write to:
Kelly Marks
Intelligent Horsemanship
Lethornes
Lambourn
Berkshire RG17 8QS

Telephone: (+44) 01488 71300 or fax: (+44) 01488 73783